WHO AM I

The Making of DAVON BROWN

ELDER DAVON BROWN

Copyright @ 2024 by Davon Brown
All right reserved
First Edition

Who Am I: The Making of Davon Brown

This book is a work of non-fiction.

Details in some anecdotes and stories have been changed to protect the identities of the people involved.

Unless otherwise indicated, all Scriptures are from the Authorized King James Version of the Bible, New King James Version of the Bible, New Living Translation of the Bible, New International Version of the Bible, The Amplified Version of the Bible, and English Standard Version of the Bible.

All rights reserved, including the right to reproduce this book or portions thereof in any form whatsoever.

Amazon: ISBN 979-8-33208-325-9 (Paperback)

DEDICATION

This book is dedicated to the glory of God, without Whom this book would not be possible. This book is also dedicated to my mother, Pastor Cynthia Brown, for her example of how to serve God and caring for me my entire life. Lastly, I dedicate this to you, the reader. This book was not written for mere enjoyment or self-satisfaction. This book serves as a testament to how God can shape one's life into His divine will and purpose.

- ELDER DAVON BROWN

CONTENTS

INTRODUCTION	7
ONE **IN THE BEGINNING**	11
TWO **MY NAME IS DAVON**	21
THREE **LITTLE CHURCH BOY**	27
FOUR **HOW WAS SCHOOL?**	33
FIVE **OF A DIFFERENT KIND**	43
SIX **I AM A PREACHER**	49
SEVEN **WHAT DOES GOD SOUND LIKE?**	57
EIGHT **LIAR LIAR, PANTS ON FIRE**	63
NINE **PUSHED TO COOK**	69
TEN **MINISTRY: PLEASURES AND MISERIES**	75
ELEVEN **OFF TO COLLEGE**	89
TWELVE **THANK YOU**	99
THIRTEEN **MIND UNDER CONSTRUCTION**	109
CONCLUSION: GOD BUILT ME INTO MYSELF	117
ABOUT THE AUTHOR	121

INTRODUCTION

Who am I? It is a question that many are still asking themselves and I am one of them. This question is so difficult to answer because we change every day. Time and circumstances change our very sense of self-being. The "answer" to "who am I" is our identity.

Our identity is our all-encompassing system of memories, experiences, feelings, thoughts, relationships, and values that define who each of us are. It is the stuff that makes up a "self." Identity is a critical part of understanding who we are. Why? Because we can break up identity into components (values, experiences, relationships). These components we can identify and understand. Then, once we have understood the components of our identity, we can get a big picture of who we are. We, as living beings, search for and find comfort in a solid sense of identity. It grounds us. It gives us confidence. And our sense of identity affects every single thing in our lives – from the choices we make to the values we live by.

Your story is what makes you unique and powerful. Take the time to reflect on your life experiences, both positive and negative. What have you learned from them? How have they shaped you? Embracing your story means accepting every part of it, even the challenging moments. By doing so, you can gain a deeper understanding of yourself and what God has in store for you.

When you find yourself, you can live authentically, being true to who you are at your core. This means embracing your strengths, accepting your weaknesses, and showing up in the world as your genuine self. Living authentically allows you to attract people and experiences that align with your true essence.

We all have thought patterns that hold us back. Take a moment to identify five problematic thought patterns that frequently persist in your life. Explore how these patterns translate into beliefs and behaviors. Be specific and give examples. Understanding the impact of these patterns on your thinking and life is crucial for creating change.

Jesus asked his disciples, "Who do men say that I am?" Many had intelligent answers but were wrong. But Peter received a revelation that Jesus is the Son of God. I believe that a vital step in finding our identity is, first, knowing who Jesus is. As Christians, our core identity is found in Jesus Himself. We are no longer separated from God but intimately joined together with Christ through His indwelling Spirit (1 Cor. 6:17). Understanding our new position, privilege, and purpose fuels us to walk worthy of the gospel as we grow into His likeness.

While we wait for the full revelation of who we are in glory, we can renew our minds to truth and live out our identities in Christ each day. By embracing who God says we are, we can experience freedom and fullness of life in Jesus.

In the absence of knowing our true selves in God, people often attempt to construct their own identities based on factors like careers, relationships, ideologies, possessions, pleasures, and even sinful lifestyles. But basing our worth and purpose on such things often leads to feelings of emptiness, anxiety, disappointment, and suffering when those things inevitably let us down.

Our identity in Christ is a transformative biblical truth with profound implications for how we live. As redeemed children of God, we are infinitely loved, eternally secure, and called to fulfill God's purposes.

To help me understand finding my identity, while in prayer,

the Spirit of God gave me a revelation of the power of His Word. James 1:21 says, "Wherefore lay apart all filthiness and superfluity of naughtiness, and receive with meekness the engrafted word, which is able to save your souls." The engrafted word describes the permanent establishment of the Word in our souls by God. The engrafting process is not necessarily a quick process, but it is a careful action with the purpose of growth.

In this book, you will go with me through some good, bad, uncomfortable, and funny times of my life. You will see how I found confidence in who I am through my life, school, and ministry. The Bible tells us that we overcome by the blood of the lamb and the words of our testimony. Since Jesus did his part, it's time for me to do mine. I overcame a lot of things such as infant health challenges, the rejection of a father, life decisions, schooling, and ministry.

This autobiography is filled with life moments, lessons, milestones, and many revelations from God that were given to me in the past 23 years. This is the story of Who I Am.

ONE

IN THE BEGINNING

"Before I formed you in the womb I knew you, before you were born, I set you apart; I appointed you as a prophet to the nations." – Jeremiah 1:4

Let me introduce myself. My name is Davon Tyree Brown. In communication class, I learned that the most important thing in communicating is stating your name. I am a 23-year-old who loves God first. I love people but can be very introverted. My favorite hobbies are graphic design, watching movies, bowling, cooking, and caring for others. I have never been a troublemaker. But rather, I was always a peacemaker, whether in the home or school. But do not get on my bad side. I love learning just as much as I love teaching. I believe that we are life learners and there will never be a moment where we stop learning. I am a first-generation college graduate and graduated from Bowie State University with a Bachelor of Science in Visual Communication and Digital Media Arts. I am the founder of my own graphic design business called Davon Brown Designs. I have been in public ministry for 11 years. But it is a great time to start at the beginning.

My childhood was a humble beginning. From the stories of my mother, her pregnancy with me was a difficult experience. In February 2001, she had an asthma attack and went to the hospital. While she was there, the technicians gave her medicine and an IV. The technician put the IV in her wrist and, immediately, she went into shock and, possibly, died. One of the church members who took her, Sister Henrietta Lee, was crying and thought my mother was gone. But my mother came through it. Now let me talk about Sister Lee. Sister Lee always asked my mother when she was having another child even though my mother wasn't married. So, I thank Sister Lee because she was waiting for me. After that situation, my mother was doing fine and drank an orange soda. After drinking the soda, she vomited. The doctor asked if she wanted to take a pregnancy test. On February 13, 2001, my mother found out she was pregnant, and Sister Lee was the first one to know.

My Initial due date was October 11, 2001. But I guess I

wanted to come earlier because I must have known that I did not want to share a birthday month with Halloween. To be honest, I do not like Halloween. My motto was: "In October, I don't want to go to any store." But back to the story.

Months later, my mother was going through some issues and went to Howard University Hospital. While she was there, I was coming out and the doctors pushed me back in. After that, one of my mother's friends asked about the hospital she was supposed to go to, which was The Columbia Hospital for Women. My mother did not want to go. She ended up staying for some weeks. Towards the time I was coming, they had to give her five shots to develop my lungs. Each shot sent an uncomfortable, burning sensation through her whole body.

My mother is now at The Colombia Hospital for Women, in Washington D.C., in a rough labor situation. I was born on Thursday, August 16, 2001, at around 5:50 am. I was four pounds and eleven ounces and undeveloped. So, they took me from my mother and placed me in an incubator. I had to receive an IV in my forehead because I needed medicine that normally was through another vein. But that was their only way of giving it to me. The doctors said that the mark would disappear over time, but I still have it. It's my reminder of God's faithfulness. When I think about it, I sometimes place my finger there and begin to thank God.

I spent a few weeks in the hospital and my mother visited all the time. She prayed and spent time with me. One Sunday, the nurse encouraged her to rest and stay home because I was alright. She went to church and sat in the back on the right side. She was there crying because she heard that her baby might die. Evangelist Sharlene Nichols, who I call my grandma in church, came to her and began to pray and restore her. During the time of her pregnancy, Evangelist Nichols, her son, Pastor Kendall Nichols, her husband, Overseer Norman Nichols, and their church was always at our church. But after the pregnancy, they stopped coming often and my mother believes that they were coming just for her and I.

This is a perfect example of the faith of a mother. A mother who believes in God against all odds. A mother's faith is generational, it leaves a legacy. A mother's faith first believes what God said in His word. And second, she believes in her children. She has been through a pregnancy without my father's help. She gave birth to me before time. And now her blessing is sick. The doctors said that I would not live. If I lived, I would have difficulty in speaking, comprehension, walking, and seeing. But she believed in God. While growing up, I remember waking out of my sleep and my pillow smelled like anointing oil. From this, I knew my mother came where I was sleeping and anointed me in the midnight hours. There were mornings when I would hear her praying and speaking in tongues. I reverenced this so much that I would stay in bed until she was done. Thank God for a praying mother.

After I left the hospital, my mother kept me close to her. I came home just a few days before the tragic 9/11 Attacks. And the first place she took me was The Church. At the time, my mom attended Greater New Foundation Full Gospel Church under the late Bishop Roscoe Harris Sr. And I will talk about him later. There was a woman named Missionary Bradley and she spoke over my life. She said, "As long as he lives, he will not want for anything." And I can testify that the word has not hit the ground. Isaiah 55:11 says, "So shall my word be that goes out from my mouth; it shall not return to me empty, but it shall accomplish that which I purpose and shall succeed in the thing for which I sent it."

My mother raised me in the faith of God. By the time I began school, she instilled in me to know God and showed me how to love him. She was my example. The first scripture she taught me, while walking to school, was Philippians 4:13: "I can do all things through Christ who strengthens me." She taught me the importance of believing in God as my strength.

This scripture is a cornerstone of my faith. This faith was engrafted in me and opposed every negative accusation that the enemy put over my life.

I grew up in a single-parent household with my older brother. I had a great upbringing. An issue was just the environment that we were near. But there was a time when it was not bad. I remember when the community had Block Parties, where they would block the entire street. Literally, it was a neighborhood cookout. I looked forward to this. Everyone came out and enjoyed each other's company while eating and dancing. You always had the elders gathered with their cards and beer and parents having fun with their children. It was an exciting time. There was a sense of community, which is hard to find these days. But I had one goal: to ride my bike down the hill. Since I knew the street was blocked, I rode my bike down the hill just to walk back up and do it again. To this day, I still do not know how to ride a bike.

We had an older neighbor next to us. His name was Mr. James. Mr. James would sit on the porch almost every evening with his Budweiser Beer. Sometimes, we would sit outside with him. After a while, I would go play in the dirt where the ant hills were. I am fascinated with ants. I was fascinated by how they walked in line, gathered food, and created a whole colony that worked together. Even if you smush an anthill, they have a whole community underground. Nothing can stop the determination of an ant. My mother did not like me doing that because I would end up dirty and needed to wash up. When I came into the house, she would say, "You smell like outside." Those were good times.

One Christmas, my mom brought me a kid's drum set. I was a musical person, especially in church. I would go outside and play my set. The thing about where our building was, the front looked like a pulpit with stairs that came to a large platform and led to our apartment doors. I broke my first drumsticks. Then, I did not have drumsticks at one point. So, what I did was this. Every time my mom brought a pair of heels, I would use the shoe sticks to play my drums. Sometimes. I snuck into the kitchen and used our kitchen utensils. That might be the reason some were missing. And my mother would sit out there with me just in case anybody wanted to start something.

There was a lady that lived in the lower abandoned part of our building. She was suffering from addiction, but she would ask my mother if I was playing my drums that day. My drum set was in the corner and next to our front room window. She would listen through the window or screen door. Also, I started preaching outside. Looking back at them moments, I realize that I started my own street ministry. My ministry started with playing drums and preaching on the porch. And my mother said, the more played the drums at the window, that was the less time the lady spent in her addiction. And I can testify that this lady is sober and has been delivered from her addiction for years. One day, a member from the church came by and saw me bringing my drums outside. Because of his knowledge of the neighborhood, he was concerned. But little did he know, I did this all the time. He asked my mother, "Are you gonna let him go outside?" And mother said, "Yeah and we are gonna sit outside with him."

Growing up, I had high hopes for my life. I thought big and prosperous thoughts. You've heard that success is a state of mind, but what does that mean? It's more than just having good intentions and putting yourself in the right place at the right time. It's about how you feel about your life and how you act on those feelings. So, if you want to succeed, start by understanding how your attitude determines your direction, actions, and decisions. Attitude plays an important role in shaping your life by determining how you see yourself and the world around you. These beliefs form the basis for all of our actions, whether they are positive or negative. Attitude affects many areas of life including work performance, family, relationships, health, happiness, and success at school or work. This is only the beginning of these amazing stories. Let me encourage you. Do not despise small beginnings!! Trust that it is just that, a beginning! No matter how your life starts, it does not compare to what God has spoken and predestined over your life. I wasn't born with the fanciest lifestyle or in the safest neighborhood. But God had a plan for my life.

Let's look at God's Word. In Genesis, no matter how dark the atmosphere was where earth would soon be, the Spirit of God was still moving. The Amplified Bible states that "The Spirit of God was moving (hovering, brooding) over the face of the waters." What does brooding mean? Brooding means to hatch, to conceive, and to plan. Even in the creation's darkest moment, God still had a plan. God had a plan for me. A plan for my life that was ascending and abundant and above anything anyone could ask or think because Philippians 4:13 shows where the power that works in me is.

Jeremiah 29:11 says, "For I know the plans I have for you," declares the Lord, "plans to prosper you and not to harm you, plans to give you hope and a future." This verse reminds us that God has a specific plan for each of our lives. He desires to bring us prosperity, hope, and a bright future. It reassures us that God is in control and has good intentions for us.

In the beginning, God created. And He created me.

TWO

MY NAME IS DAVON

> *"But now thus says the Lord, he who created you, O Jacob, he who formed you, O Israel: "Fear not, for I have redeemed you; I have called you by name, you are mine." – Isaiah 43:1*

Our name is the first component that shapes who we are. Names are important. They shape our identities. They define us. The first piece of information strangers learn about most people is a name picked for them by their parents. But what we are called can have a surprising impact on how others perceive us.

Your name can be associated with honor and heroism, or your name can develop a bad reputation. The expression to "make a name for yourself" points to this very human aspiration to be known, to be recognized, to achieve recognized goals, and to "be somebody." Your name is important because it is tied to your history, your reputation, and your future.

You might have dwelt on the different ways that your parents shaped you – from their warmth and strictness to their generosity and pushiness. But perhaps you haven't thought so much about the consequences of one particularly important gift they bestowed upon you – your name – and whether you like it, and how society views it.

Parents often agonize over what to call their children. It can feel like a test of creativity or a way to express their own personalities or identities through their offspring. But what many parents might not fully realize is that the choice they make over their children's names could play a part in shaping how others see their child and therefore ultimately the kind of person their child becomes.

I must admit something. While growing up, some part of me did not like the name "Davon." As a surprise, my first name came from my father, who was not fairly present for much of my life. Who is "Davon? Why would you name me that? And for what purpose? He named me. I loved my middle name, which is Tyree, more than my first name. Now, do not get me wrong. "Davon" is not a bad name. I realized that the problem was not the name. But I did not like it because of who gave it to me.

For years I wondered, how could you be in my life long enough to name me but not be there for me as I grew up. I told my mom, "When I get older, I am going to change my name." On top of that, some people did not pronounce it correctly. It is pronounced "duh-von" not "day-von." I should have added that earlier, but now you have it.

In my childhood, my relationship with my father was unfavorable. I knew who he was, but his presence was not constant. No graduations, fewer than five birthdays, no personal outings, or words of affirmation. When I was younger, the only time I went over to his house was if I asked but I was never invited. On his side, I am the sixth child of nine children. Unfortunately, I am part of the group that never lived with him. I was fortunate to meet the two brothers that were after me. I enjoyed playing with them because, on my mother's side, my brother was eleven years older and not home a lot. So, I grew up as if I were the only child even though I had a sibling. My two brothers, on my father's side, were the main reason I asked to come over. My visits were fun with my brothers, but I did not feel welcome. I felt like I was just another person in the house, not a son.

I was never asked: What is your favorite color? How's

school? What is your favorite meal? What do you like to do? I felt like I did not exist in his world. He had a wife, and she wasn't welcoming. It was just an occasional "Hey," but nothing more than that. There was a time when food was cooked, and she told us to come and eat. I wasn't hungry and asked for a small bag of chips. She went and told my father, and this small gesture turned into a huge problem. Just because I wasn't hungry.

My brothers and I loved WWE. My favorite wrestler was The Undertaker. We would go to the back room and wrestle each other while watching reruns. But there were moments when my father and his wife would get into loud arguments. When I was there, I would take my brothers to the back room and turn up the TV so they wouldn't hear. Now, I wasn't there all the time, and I don't know what they experienced during those altercations. In those moments, I took the role of a protective big brother. But still, on the inside, I envied them because they had him and I didn't.

Many nights, I questioned how he could sleep not knowing my well-being. We would see him in stores and restaurants and the interaction would be so weird and uncomfortable for me. My mother would force me to call him on his birthday and Father's Day every year, even though I did not want to. And back then, texting was not as popular. Every Sunday, we rode past his house because the route to our church took us past there. I would look out the window just to see his white truck. But one night, I was going over to his house, and he went into a store. I stayed in the car, and I called my mother. I told her that I did not feel like I was supposed to be there. My mother was ready to come and get me, but I stayed to see my brothers. That weekend was my last visit. My mind got to the point that I didn't care if he died because he became nonexistent to me. If he had died during this time, I was not going to the funeral. Who would want to go to the funeral of a parent and people barely know you? I didn't want to go through that feeling like a black sheep.

Rejection is a terrible feeling for a child. And growing up with it was a struggle. From the rejection of my father, I started rejecting myself. I missed awesome opportunities because I found every reason why I wasn't qualified. But through Christ, I found God to be my father.

My relationship with God is important because I needed God to be my father. He presents Himself as a Father because we all know what a Father is and does. Even if we did not have earthly fathers who treated us well, we have an intrinsic understanding of what a good father should be. God planted that understanding in our hearts. We all have a need to be loved, cherished, protected, and valued. Ideally, an earthly father will meet those needs. But even if he doesn't, God will. Psalm 27:10 says, "When my father and my mother forsake me, then the Lord will take me up." The places in my life where my father forsook me, God continued to fill every place that I needed to become who I am today. God sent godly men into my life to impart in me. I gleaned from their lives and observed how they loved their families, church, and even themselves.

The book of Revelation tells us that we will get a new name. For the rest of our lives—here and in the afterlife—we will be getting to know more about the name of our great God. God heals people in his name. We are taught to pray in his name. We are to revere his name and bring glory to his name. We are not to take God's name in vain. God's name matters, and so does yours. Knowing who we are will help us to reflect God's name.

My name is Davon. Not because my father gave it to me, but because this is the name that God is using for His glory. God may not have changed my name like people in the bible. But he changed how I see it. It is not where my name came from, but it is all about what God formed it to be.

THREE

LITTLE CHURCH BOY

"Surely goodness and mercy shall follow me all the days of my life: and I will dwell in the house of the LORD forever." – Psalm 23:6

Can I get an Amen? I love the church. Other than school, church was another source of community that I loved. I mentioned earlier that the first place my mother took me when I was born, was the church. I grew up in Greater New Foundation Full Gospel Church under the leadership of the late Bishop Roscoe Harris Sr. Even as a baby, I was quiet, settled, and observant. My upbringing in church was a peculiar experience for my mother. The hand of God was upon me. According to my mother, I would get up early every morning at 5 AM to watch Joyce Myers preach and go back to sleep. And I did this for a long time.

As I got older, I was always attentive. I did not make any noise or went to sleep. I was attentive to the preacher. I was not too excited about the singing, but my interest sparked when the Word of God was coming from Bishop Roscoe Harris. Around ages six and seven, I started moving to the front of the church. Then, I would go home and talk about the service. I would tell my mother things that she might not see or get. I got a notebook and began to take notes on the sermons and study my bible. I loved studying God's word so much that I would take my bible and notebook to the laundry mat, and even school.

Back in the day, I loved getting toys from McDonald's. I would use the toys to create my own church on my dresser. So, every time I left church, I would get my toys and mimic what I saw. One time, I was playing with my toys and pretended to knock one of them out in the Spirit. In a real church, this is equivalent to experiencing the power of God through the laying on of hand. Well, my mother told this story to one of her friends and she was astonished. A little time later, her friend came to my mother and told her that, when she went to church, she felt God in such a way that she fell out in the Spirit. This was another sign that God's hand was on my life.

Being a single mother can be a challenging thing. Taking care of two boys: one is a toddler, and the other is older. According to my mother, there were moments when she was feeling down about a situation. I would come to her and say, "Everything is going to be alright." She wondered, "How can he say that?" Because I did not know what was going on. Yet, the God in me knew and He used me to encourage my mother.

One service, Dr. Charlene Monk, a female preacher known in the DMV, came to Greater New Foundation. According to my mother, she called me up after she preached. She took me and sat me on her lap, and she sang a song she always sang, "Something Special Is Gonna Happen to You."

Let me talk about my inspiration: Bishop Roscoe Harris Sr. Before I was born, my mom did not know my gender. She hoped for a girl and was going to name her Raven Marie Brown. But Bishop R. Harris told my mother that as long as she conceives, she will never have a girl. So, here I came. He knew a portion of who I was before my own mother. Even though my mother did not conceive me through marriage, He never condemned her. She never stood in the church for confession. The only thing Bishop R. Harris did was preach God's word. In fact, the church was excited for her and more excited when I came.

Andrew B. Newberg, an American neuroscientist, authored a book called, "How God Changes Your Brain." In an excerpt I read, he mentioned that "Young children see God as a face because their brains cannot process abstract spiritual concepts." After reading that, it brought understanding to my initial relationship with God. In my youth, Bishop R. Harris was the symbol of God that I honored. I honored him so much until I thought I had to change my last name to Harris in order to preach. That is how much I love this man.

My love for ministry started through his life. He was humble and knowledgeable in the Word of God. I gleaned from his life. And he knew that I was going to be someone great. And his wife, Overseer Annie M. Harris, always called me her Junior Bishop. On Tuesday, December 7th, 2010, he passed away. I was crushed because the man I looked up to was gone. My mother waited until I got home from school to tell me. A part of me was gone. I remember that when he died, Deitrick Haddon's "Well Done" came on the radio so much. To this day, I cannot listen to that song because it takes me back to that moment.

Our relationship was like an Elijah and Elisha moment. Even though I was not around him personally, his anointing was imparted in me to carry out God's work. I am forever grateful for Bishop Roscoe Harris because this church boy found God through him.

I started playing the drums in church. There was a certain face I made when I knew I was playing them well. In 2011, I started practicing on the keyboard, not knowing how far it would take me. The first song I was taught was "Lean on Me." But I started listening to the music from my favorite gospel song. I learned how to play the keyboard by myself. Now, I'm not perfect, but I can get the job done. There was a set of twins that I played instruments with during our church services. We would alternate which instrument we would play. Their mother started getting to church earlier just so her kids could play the drums or keyboard instead of me. But I still ended up playing because they didn't want to play without me. Their mother took it so far as to embarrass me at an important service. The church was full of people. My mom knew she was going to do something. She told someone to get on the drums while I was there playing. I was pushed off and I sat next to the drums crying. Now, let me tell you something about my grandmother. My grandmother doesn't play about me. She calls me by my middle name. She got out of her seat and walked to the front of the church where I was. She asked, "Tyree, you alright?" I told her "Yes" because if I had said no, the service would have been over. Sometime later, their mother apologized for what she did, and I accepted it. I was so determined to serve God, and I picked up anything that I could. I even got a bass guitar just to be able to play, which I don't play anymore. That was just a placeholder.

The church can be messy sometimes – the sermon may be boring, the song leader might be tone-deaf, and there might be no one else your age there. But you know what? God works powerfully in messy, unimpressive churches; he uses them to build disciples and to show his glory. I love church most of all because I trust and know that God is working awesomely through it. I love the church. I confess to that. I am a confirmed lover of the church. It thrills me beyond anything and everything to serve the church. It is the supreme joy of my life to labor for the church. To spend my years on behalf of the church, I wouldn't trade for anything.

FOUR

HOW WAS SCHOOL?

"Education is the most powerful weapon which you can use to change the world." – Nelson Mandela

How was school? A question that most children hear their parents ask. School was an important part of my life. I was an amazing student and had a hunger to learn. I have a lot of memories from my school years, but I will get to college later in the book.

I began my early education at Peaches and Cream Child Development Center. My mother caught the bus to take me to daycare. She took me to the daycare and got back on the bus to go to her job. But she struggled during the winter season. Her frustration came from my father because he hung around near the neighborhood we lived in and had a car. My great-uncle, Uncle

Plunk, met us at the bus stop and carried me on his neck. God favored my mother and I that her co-worker volunteered to take her to get me. He left work at 2 pm, went home to pick up his wife, went back to the job and picked up my mother at 5 pm, took her to get me, and took us home. So, God always provided for us.

My daycare was called Peaches and Cream Child Development Center. My daycare teacher was Ms. Rainy. As far as I remember, she was an older lady and very kind to us. We went on many field trips and Sister Lee went with me on one of them. But my mother had a friend that she grew up with. Let's call her Tammy. Tammy lived over us and struggled with addiction, but she was a huge help in our lives. According to my mother, she used to wait until my mother and I got into the house safely. Tammy went on a few field trips with me. But God favored me so much that Tammy would not do drugs the day before the field trip. She cleaned herself up as if she were clean and went with me on the field trip. So, I had an impact on people's lives just by existing. This is another person who forsook their addiction for me.

On graduation day, I had a breakdown. I was so scared to sing, speak, and stand in front of the audience. God made a way for my mother to buy my white suit and white shoes. My family, church, including Bishop R. Harris, were there. But little did they know I was losing it in the back. I was crying in the back because I did not want to go out there. I got myself together just to go out there, get scared again, and sit in the front row with my mom for the entire graduation ceremony. Isn't that something? But I believe that everyone has their own moment with stage fright.

My next step was elementary school. I went to Arts and Technology Academy PCS, which was within walking distance from our home. Arts and Technology Academy was a great school, and I believe that it was before its time. We had a huge field and playgrounds. On the third floor, we had a library and computer lab that was accessible. Huge auditorium and cafeteria. The downfall was the neighborhood. I can't even count how many lockdowns we had. I started in kindergarten, and I had the kindest teacher. Let's name her Ms. Bee. Ms. Bee was middle-aged and light-skinned. The first couple of days I cried every time my mother left me. It is not easy starting over again. But I made some friends and was comfortable leaving my mother to go to class.

In first grade, I had an opportunity to be in a school play. Our school produced "101 Dalmatians". The school let all the first graders be Dalmatians. ATA was known for our creativity. As I reminisce, the school thrived in arts, music, dance, and productions. Most of our productions were at a theater called THEARC- pronounced "The Ark." I got the opportunity to work as a stage crew member with our Physical Education Teacher.

When you're young, it's not hard to make friends. My main friends were Emmanuel, Zai, Davon Powell, and Jordan. There were many others, but they were the ones I mainly talked to. Emmanuel lived across from the school. One time, we had a sleepover at his house. I was the last one to arrive. I opened the door, and the lights were off and quiet. I was stuck and confused. Suddenly, everyone came from behind couches and around corners, while attacking me with Nerf guns. We laughed it off and had a great time. Another time, I let Emmanuel borrow one of my Nintendo Wii games. During that era, Nintendo Wii was very popular, and every kid had one. On the way home, I stopped by his house to pick up the game. As I walked to the car, I was urged to check inside the case. I opened it and the game wasn't in there. Kindly, I walked back to the door, and he gave me the game. We laughed about it the next day at school because I caught him. Those were awesome times.

I remember the time I got suspended. Our school didn't allow us to bring toys to school. One day, I snuck in my "Bee Movie" toys. If you don't know what that is, look it up. We were playing on the playground, and I had them in my black hat. While playing with one of my friends, I struck him on the head by accident. I believe the only reason I got in trouble was because the teacher heard him crying on the playground. I was sent to the office, and they suspended me for one school day.

But let's talk about second grade. In second grade, a lot of events happened. Have you ever wondered why I wear glasses and how

I got to this point? In simple words, I put my friend's glasses on. A couple of days later, my vision started getting blurry, and, over winter break, I got glasses. In addition, I made another friend. His name was Sean. Sean was a tricky person with mood swings. Sometimes he wanted to be friends and other times not to be friends. One day, he came up with the idea of tying both of his shoes together. And what did I do? Tied mines together too. Imagine me hopping down those stairs to the principal's office so they could cut my shoelaces loose.

I loved my class my teacher was amazing. She was my first-grade teacher too. My favorite time was recess. But when it rained, we had indoor recess. And for some reason, my teacher didn't allow me to play and made me sit at my desk. I was so angry that I kicked my desk. Later that day, I was in aftercare, and we went outside. One of the faculty members came and got me from the playground to ask some questions. They took me upstairs to the classroom and the classroom was trashed. There were toys, blocks, and paper everywhere. Immediately, I started crying saying, "I would never do this!" Nobody was there to defend me. People were screaming at me because they believed I did this. They took me to the security room and played a video showing the person they thought was me. A lady named Ms. Benton came into the room and looked at the footage. Immediately, she said, "That's Sean." Sean went into the classroom after school and tore up the classroom. The stupid part is that Sean had cornrows, and I had a regular haircut. At the time, I didn't have glasses. My teacher thought it was me based on my little behavior during recess. I was framed! Guilty before proven innocent.

    They returned me to the playground with my aftercare teacher, Ms. Johnson. When my mother picked me up, Ms. Johnson told her about the situation and my mother was furious. How would you feel about your child being interrogated and no one contacts you? You'll be furious too. My mother went to my teacher and asked, "What if a child went home and told their parent you molested them? What would you do?" After that, I came to school and told my friends. But I never had a problem with that teacher again.

    One school day, I had a bad cough. I still went to school, but I spent the whole day coughing. After school, I went home, threw up, and began to have an asthma attack. My mother called the paramedics, and the ambulance came to the house. The paramedics didn't want to take me for some odd reason. My mother urged them to take me because I vomited too. I ended up in Children's Hospital for some days while they ran tests and gave me medicine. I received coloring pages and played some games while I was there. It was like a free vacation, just in a hospital. When I finally walked out of the room, I made a friend who was on the same floor as me. But of course, my time was up. Time sure passes by when you're having fun.

During the school year, I looked forward to the quarterly book fairs. Book fairs were awesome, and my mother always gave me money for them. I loved the award ceremonies. I received so many awards over the years. I got perfect attendance, writing awards, math awards, and most improved. Reports cards were scary moments, especially the ones that came out before Christmas break. Those report cards determined if you were getting gifts or not. Multiple kids did their best during that quarter just for the gifts and flunked their grades for the rest of the school year.

In third grade, my teacher was Ms. Scott. Ms. Scott was tall, skinny, and dark-skinned. Ms. Scott was nice but was a strict teacher. She had lots of wooden yardsticks she used to get certain students' attention. There were times when she whacked the yardstick so hard on the desk, it would break. She was nice to me because I was a part of the group that behaved well.

Now, fourth grade was tricky because my teacher was an angel in disguise. Her name was Ms. Harper. Ms. Harper was a nice person in the beginning, but things quickly changed. She always went around the school singing Vashawn Mitchell's "Nobody Greater." She would always nitpick things about our projects. She even said I was stubborn. At the time, I didn't know what the word "stubborn" meant. After looking up the meaning, I never consider myself a stubborn person. Maybe it was my confidence that was a threat. One project, she accused me of not having a map key on my poster board. I told her the map key was on there. She found it but I guess because of my tone, she wanted to have a meeting with my mother. My mother came upstairs and came to the classroom. Ms. Harper began to talk about my behavior. Something in me caused me to assert myself. I told Ms. Harper, "I heard what you said because I have an ear like a dog!" Where did that come from? I couldn't tell you. This was the first moment I ever stood up for myself.

Even though I went through these things, I never had bad grades and respected my teachers. In fifth grade, we had the opportunity to write memoir books. We had to choose five memories to write about. One day, our teacher came to class with the box containing the books we made. Everyone received their book except me. I was concerned and started getting upset. But little did I know, my book was on display in the school. That was such an honor for me.

Another opportunity I had in elementary school was a financial literacy program in fifth grade. They taught us about checking and saving accounts, deposits, and withdrawals, and how to write a check. They even gave us our own checkbook. Towards the end of the program, they took us to a place called BizTown. BizTown was an interactive town where we ran businesses and careers. I was the mayor of BizTown for the day. The only thing I did was give a speech, went to all the businesses, and got free stuff.

I had a lot of friends in school. Our favorite activity was going to the computer lab to play games, especially Poptropica. In our math class, we would play games while we were supposed to do work. But I was different. I did my work and then I played games. So, when the others got in trouble, I had my work finished. At my elementary school graduation, I received a $50 scholarship for good sportsmanship in physical education and multiple awards. My elementary school experience was amazing with inspiring teachers and faculty.

During them years, I developed a love for teaching. While I don't desire to be a schoolteacher, my anointing includes the operation of The Teacher in the five-fold ministry. I loved teaching so much that I used to teach the GED students at my mother's job. I would make math worksheets, and they always looked forward to me coming to the class. Currently, I teach the word of God with passion because my goal is to move God's people out of ignorance and into wisdom.

Another thing I loved about school was the summer camps. ATA held annual summer camps for the students. We had academics in the morning and played in the afternoon. In the afternoon, we alternated activities based on our grades. We alternated between Physical Education, Art, Dance, and Recess. We had a game room, and my favorite game was Dance Dance Revolution. One year, we had a cooking course where we made banana and peanut butter sandwiches. It was good, but I can't eat them anymore since I am allergic to peanuts now. We went on a field trip every week. The trips were either the skating rick or swimming pool. One time at the swimming pool, I almost drowned. There was a rope that separated us little kids from the deep side of the pool. My "adventurous" self decided to step on the platform and get in the deep side. I got in twice while holding the platform and made it out. I thought I was doing something. But the third time, my hand slipped, and I started drowning. I was trying to grab the platform but couldn't reach it. Nobody saw my little self because I was behind the platform. Thanks be to God that I managed to grab it because I would have been a goner. At the end of summer camp, we always ended it by going to Six Flags America. I have awesome memories of my early education and wouldn't change anything.

How was school? School was great!!

FIVE

OF A DIFFERENT KIND

"Don't be afraid of being different, be afraid of being the same as everyone else." – Unknown Author.

It is easy to compare yourself to others and worry about living up to society's expectations. Sometimes it's hard being different from family members, coworkers, schoolmates, or friends. Those who try to blend in with others are truly taking the easy route; they aren't required to think their own thoughts, so they just end up going with the flow. Being different by thinking outside of the box is what has helped many people become great leaders, inventors, entrepreneurs, and innovators.

In my youth, I constantly heard people say, "He's strange." Especially, one of my uncles. The men in my family were into sports, even my brother had experience in sports. But I was an inside person. I loved church, art, and computers. I was a peaceful person and never gave anyone any problems. But there were times when I asked God why He made me like this. I didn't ask this question because I didn't like who I was. But everyone, at some point, has the desire to be accepted and understood. I did not understand how people around me could express themselves with anger with ease, but I felt like I couldn't express that. I have always been slow to anger. Now, I've gotten upset many times but never enraged. There were characteristics and interests I had that I didn't understand because the people around me did not have them. Other than my mother and grandmother, there was nobody else in my family that went to church. There were no other artists or computer geeks. There were times I felt like an outcast towards the male side of my immediate family.

 I remember a time when my mother would introduce me to her friends, and I didn't want to speak. I didn't know them. They were her friends or her co-workers. Now don't get me wrong, there were some that I was comfortable around and talked to. But new people were a huge no. According to my mother, there was a time she introduced me to somebody, and I didn't want to speak. She told me to say hello because that was her friend. I responded, "That's your friend, not mine."

Even in church, I was different. It was rare for me to sit with the other children because they didn't pay attention like I did. They played and laughed while I sat in the front row, listening to the preacher. One time, the usher told me I couldn't sit in the front row and forced me to sit with the other children. I didn't care what Pastor was coming, it's my church and I'm sitting on the front row. I loved my bible. In 2010, my mom gave me a NIV VeggieTales Bible for kids. I wrote and highlighted in that bible and carried it everywhere.

Even though I maneuvered my way into finding myself and embracing my differences, there were moments when I felt lonely. The only source of community I had at the time was school because that was the place where I could be around kids my age. I remember a time when we were living with my grandmother. And I started feeling lonely. The devil whispered to me, "Run away." But I was strong enough to defeat him with God's word because where was I going to go? Sometime later, the devil came back with loneliness and said, "Run away and go to the train track down the street." Now, I didn't want to die or take my life. I just wanted someone to play with because school was out. Allow me to pivot. The devil will always bring an idea, thought, or suggestion in your most vulnerable moments. Most of his suggestions don't make sense. When Jesus was tempted in the wilderness, the devil didn't come until Jesus came to a vulnerable and unsatisfied place in his flesh. Jesus was hungry so the devil challenged his identity by suggesting to turn the stone into bread. But Jesus used the word of God to combat the enemy. It is written. When the enemy comes to plant his seed in your mind, you must have a "it is written" in your spirit. Because of my relationship with God, He gave me the strength through His word to combat the enemy's plan.

Look at David. David was the youngest of his brothers. When Samuel came to anoint one of Jessie's sons, David was not present. David was sent to the field to watch over the sheep. His family did not consider him as an option because he was different. Isn't that something? David wasn't considered. You will go through things in your life where people will not consider you. Your name will never hit their mind. And if it hits their mind, they will never give you the opportunity. But God considered David. He was not physically strong like his brother. But little did they know, David had an inner strength from God. This is why the Lord told Samuel not to look on the outside, but God sees the inside of a person.

As we go about our daily lives, we are bombarded by

pressures from our peers, from the media, and from society as a whole. They tell us we should look a certain way, act a certain way, and hide what makes us unique. We shouldn't try to fit into a mold created by those around us. God created us to be different. We came with a unique body and face, soul and heart, passions and dreams, goals, and a purpose. We shouldn't do things because we think they will make us cool, appreciated, popular, or successful. We should choose our words and actions based on what is right and what passions God has implanted within our hearts.

What we don't understand most of the time is this: if we are who we're meant to be instead of being someone others want us to be, we will change the world. If we become who we are created to be, we encourage others to be their true self. Others' opinions seem less important when you view a person shining their own light. They make the right decisions, care for other people, and do not live solely for the crowd's approval. Your appearance, popularity, and level of success will fade into the background when you see an individual with self-worth not dependent on any of those aspects. When you see someone loving themselves just the way they are, including their flaws, it gives you the courage to do the same. It inspires you to change the world by first loving yourself and then accepting others with all their imperfections.

Change the way you view yourself and you will change the way you view other people. Be yourself and change the world.

SIX

I AM A PREACHER

"The Spirit of the Lord God is upon me; because the Lord hath anointed me to preach good tidings unto the meek; he hath sent me to bind up the brokenhearted, to proclaim liberty to the captives, and the opening of the prison to them that are bound;" – Isaiah 61:1

What is a calling? A calling is a deep-seated sense of purpose and direction that guides our life and work choices. It is something that calls out to us and makes us feel appreciated and fulfilled. It is also something that we enjoy doing so much that we lose track of time and feel passionate about. A calling is more than just a job or a career; it is a pursuit that has a greater purpose than ourselves.

There is no doubt that preaching is a noble calling and one

that is important to God. Preaching is not simply a time-filler in the worship service, nor is it the sharing of personal experiences, no matter how emotionally stirring. Nor is it a well-organized "talk" designed to give a series of steps to a better life. Preaching, as the apostle Paul records, is the vehicle by which the life-giving truth of the gospel of Jesus Christ is conveyed. The words of the preacher are to be faithful to the Word of God, which is "the power unto salvation for everyone who believes" (Romans 1:16).

I recognized my calling to preach because I developed a love for the word of God. I used to preach to my stuffed animals. That was my first congregation. I would shout, dance, and lay hands on the stuffed animals. I used my bathrobe as a preaching robe. I used our CD player for the choir songs and praise breaks. This was before YouTube and Bluetooth Speakers. Whatever I preached in the house, I would go and preach on the porch. I was never ashamed of God.

At the time my ministry started, my mother and I attended Gethsemane Bible Center. The pastors were Bishop Linwood Harris and Pastor Stephanie Harris. My mother was on the ministerial staff and preached frequently with other ministers. Bishop Linwood Harris played an inspirational role in my life. In fact, Bishop Linwood is Bishop Roscoe Harris' brother.

Even though I couldn't have quality time with Bishop Roscoe, God did it through Bishop Linwood. He was so full of wisdom, and I soaked it all in. We went bowling together and I rode in his car. He was the person who introduced me to coffee. He was funny but corny at the same time.

In September 2013, I received my first ministering opportunity at our church. My godmother and another member planned a service for Pastor Stephanie Harris's birthday. They put in the work for me to be the preacher that day. Some members didn't think it was a wise Idea. Why him? Why didn't you get the pastor's sister? But my godmother went to Bishop Linwood, and he was more than fine with me preaching. After they got his word and approval, there was nothing that any could say. I was preaching that day. I was 12 years old at the time. This reminded me of Jesus's ministry. According to the Gospel of Luke, Jesus began His public ministry when He was about 30 years old. However, at the age of 12, Jesus stayed behind in the Temple and amazed the rabbis and teachers with his understanding. For this moment, I pulled out all my notebooks with the messages that God had given me in my private studies. I had so many notebooks because I would write on a couple of pages and move to another book.

Let me pivot for a moment. The first word God ever gave

me was from a Disney movie, "The Lion King 1 ½." The word was "Look Beyond What You See." In the movie, Timon the meerkat wanted a better life because he was an outcast in his meerkat community. The wise monkey comes in his most desperate time for direction and tells Timon, "Look beyond what you see." I heard God through this movie and went to His word. I went to Psalm 121. Psalm 121:1 says, "I will lift up my eyes to the hills— From whence comes my help? My help comes from the LORD, Who made heaven and earth." To this day, I have never ministered that sermon, but it has grounded my faith in looking past my present and into what God has for me. No matter what you go through, there is a God beyond your situation.

For this service, I was seeking God for a word, and I started listening to a song. The song was *A Word for Me* by Charles Jenkins and Fellowship Chicago. There was a verse that said, "I picked up my old bible and turned to Daniel chapter three I turned to those old Hebrew boys so they could encourage me they stepped in the fire with no doubt knowing the Lord would bring them out that's their story and that's a word for me." Immediately, I had a word, "Faith in the Fire."

Now, I had some opposition for that word. I hope you don't think that the enemy takes it easy on young kids. No, he does not. One day, I came home from school and had an awesome day. I started playing my Nintendo Wii. Later, it was time for me to get in the tub and wash for the next day. The only thing I remember is I got in the tub. Apparently, I got in the tub, got comfortable, and I went to sleep. In the apartment with lived in, the bathroom was conjoined with the two bedrooms. My grandmother got off the phone and started calling me and I didn't answer. Immediately, my mother rushed from the front room to the bathroom and found me sleeping and almost under the water. According to my mother, the water was almost at my nose. The strength of God got in her, and she lifted me out of the water. The only thing I knew was I was standing up and wet.

For the service, I wanted to wear my mother's white and purple robe. It was the same robe she wore for her initial sermon at Greater New Foundation in 2006. I preached on September 15, 2013, and shared that testimony. Everyone was so proud and enjoyed the message, even the ones that didn't want me to do it. Bishop Linwood Harris was so proud that he allowed me to serve communion that day. Sister Lee came to the service. She gifted me with a bible and case to go with it. I use that bible to this day. I've used that bible so much that I reglued the spine back in place.

I preached that message 11 years ago and it was the first public message that God gave me to present to His people. Not knowing that this message would soon ignite my walk with God in ministry. I realize that this word has a greater weight on my life compared to when I first ministered it. I have been through experiences that felt like fiery trails. I've encountered people who acted like fiery darts. I have been through the fire of rejection. I have been through the fire of family debris. I have been through a fire of sickness. I had an asthma attack at a young age and years later suffered from a rare case of tonsillitis, where I was bleeding from my tonsils. I have been through a fire of disrespect. I've been through a fire of discouragement. But God allowed me to experience the fire that I preached about to know Him.

This was the start of my public ministry. I couldn't wait for the journey that God had for me. After this moment, I read a passage of scripture. It was James 1:5-6. It says, "If any of you lacks wisdom, let him ask of God, who gives to all liberally and without reproach, and it will be given to him. But let him ask in faith, with no doubting, for he who doubts is like a wave of the sea driven and tossed by the wind." This scripture is so powerful because God is willing to give us wisdom freely. I live the part that says, "without reproach." You don't need a background check for God's wisdom because it is free. In my prayer time, I asked God for His wisdom. Ever since then, He has given me the Spirit of Wisdom, which is more than being smart and knowledgeable. God taught me that knowledge becomes wisdom when it is applied to your life. Everything that I teach others must, first, be proven effective in my life.

During them years, I always looked forward to our yearly fellowships. Yearly fellowships were services where other churches came around the same time of year. In 2015, there was a certain church that we had a yearly fellowship with every February. While the preacher was preaching, I could feel the anointing from the pulpit. At this time, I had these thin glasses with tape on the side and a Kindle tablet. She was preaching under a mighty anointing, and I was overwhelmed with the Spirit of God. She said "Say Yes" about three times, and I responded with the congregation. When I said "Yes" the third time, the power of God knocked me to the floor without anyone around me. When I got up, she prophesied these words: "Everybody, remember his name because God will do great things in his life. God has put a seal on you, and you belong to Him. And when He comes back, He's coming back for you."

Two months later, my mother and I went to Smithfield, North Carolina to support another ministry we knew. We walked to the entrance of the church and an old church mother was standing outside the door. She looked at me and said, "It's in your forehead." At the time, I was so confused. I did not know what she was talking about, but I accepted it. The next month, I was studying the book of Revelation, which is one of my favorite books in the bible. I was studying about The Third Heaven. I came across a scripture in Revelation 14 that says, "Then I looked, and behold, the Lamb was standing on Mount Zion, and with Him one hundred and forty-four thousand, having His name and the name of His Father written on their foreheads." The seal of God is God's mark of identification or ownership. It guarantees your eternal safety and certifies that your relationship with God is real.

God owns me. Now I understand the phrase that "my life is not my own." There's a deep sense that we want to belong to ourselves in a deep and meaningful way. But as Christians, we don't belong to ourselves. We belong to God. And when we walk in that mindset, we can experience an unprecedented amount of freedom. This was another indication that the calling of God was on me. I am not a motivational speaker. I am not a life coach. I am not an influencer. I am a preacher of the gospel.

SEVEN

WHAT DOES GOD SOUND LIKE?

"My sheep hear My voice, and I know them, and they follow Me." – John 10:27

Perhaps one of the most important things for Christians to understand is God's voice. Jesus even placed special emphasis on this. Here is what he said: "My sheep listen to my voice; I know them, and they follow me." Since God's guidance is critical to following him, it befits us to learn how to hear the voice of God. It is crucial to your Christian Walk.

When we ask how to hear the voice of God, we must first understand what that even means. Does it mean going up to a mountain like Moses and hearing God's audible voice with thunder and lightning, like in the old Bible movies? Or can it be something we listen for in little moments all the time?

Hearing the voice of God means you are listening for God's leading, God's direction, and God's instruction. You are inviting God into the choices and decisions of your daily life and then following his lead. This can happen in various ways and at distinct moments, but because you are in a relationship with God, it should be a part of your walk with him. Hearing God's voice can be a tricky thing. He relays Himself to us in different ways. The way one hears God is not the way another does. My question growing up was how to hear God. What does God's voice sound like? Since my mother is a prophet, I often asked her to describe the voice of God. Does He come in your ears or what? Most of the time, she couldn't describe it fully to me because that was the way God spoke to her. There were moments I could hear my mother calling me, "Davon." I would run to her and ask if she called my name. But she didn't. It happened a couple of times and the same thing happened. She did not call my name.

One day, I read the story about the prophet Samuel. Samuel was special from childhood. His story shows us the importance of listening to God's voice and obeying it at all costs. In Samuel's youth, the Lord spoke to him and called his name. Samuel thought it was Eli, who was a priest and a judge of the Israelites in the city of Shiloh and became Samuel's guardian after Hannah brought her son to the temple. Samuel runs to Eli asking if he was called. But Eli said no. When God called him in the night, of course, Samuel thought it was Eli. He was used to obeying, just like me, so he got up right away. This happened three times, and finally, Eli understood that God was trying to speak to the young boy. So, he told Samuel that when he heard the voice again to answer, "Speak Lord, for your servant is listening."

Sometimes, we miss our moment of hearing God because we compare our experience with other's experience. It's ok to ask others for guidance but be open to the many ways God speaks. In the last chapter, I told you that God spoke to me through a gospel song and kids' movies. As I grew older, I developed my spiritual ears. Later God taught me that my spiritual ears were not on the outside but on the inside. God channels His word in me, not to me. I remember instances where I prophesied to every single person in one service and the words just came out of my mouth. I didn't hear anything and then said something. He just talked through me. Ezekiel 3:27 says, "But when I speak with you, I will open your mouth, and you shall say to them, 'Thus says the Lord GOD.'"

God gave me a revelatory illustration in explaining how He talks to me and how I hear Him. Let's say you have a wireless printer. This printer has abilities that can be done by itself, such as copying. However, the printer cannot produce a document unless there is another source that sends it. Where is the document? The document is on your computer, laptop, or tablet. Your device has all the seen and unseen information about your document. Information such as words, pictures, page numbers, and color. It even holds electronic codes that only IT workers can find. So, your device has the information, and the printer can produce the tangible version of the information. But something is missing. A connection. The printer will never receive that information if there is no internet connection. With this connection, our device and printer must be on the same connection. When this connection is successful, the moment you press print on your device, the information will travel to the printer through the connection, and it will produce exactly what it looks like on the device. God is the device, and I am the printer. God holds all the information I need, but I must be connected to hear Him.

There is one more thing for you to consider as you learn how to hear the voice of God. As I mentioned before, God does not just speak through his word. Sometimes, you sense God is leading you to do something or go in a specific direction, and you are unsure. In these cases, God may use someone or something outside of you to confirm what you believe God is saying. Let me give you some ways this could happen. You could be in church, and the pastor preaches the exact thing you felt God was speaking to your heart. Someone could pray for you and, without you telling them anything, they pray the exact thing God put in your heart. A friend could call you and share the exact thing God had placed in your heart, which confirms he was speaking to you. In situations like these, what is important is the exact nature and precision of what happened. These should not be general things that could apply to anyone but specific things that apply to your situation. They may even be things only you and God know about. When things like this happen, they can be a way of confirming you are indeed hearing the voice of God.

Learning how to hear the voice of God is something you will do for the rest of your life. As you continue in prayer and his word, you will distinguish his voice from the multitudes of other voices, including yours. As a guiding principle, God will never lead you to do anything that contradicts his word or leads you into sin. However, he wants to speak to you, and he wants to guide you through this life. He will primarily do that through his word, but remember: He's a living God, and he still speaks.

Our job is to learn how to listen and find out how He's talking to us.

EIGHT

LIAR LIAR, PANTS ON FIRE

"Truthful lips endure forever, but a lying tongue is but for a moment." – Proverbs 12:19

Everyone has lied before. Even me. People lie for a variety of reasons, such as to avoid receiving punishment, obtain rewards, or keep personal information secret. Trust is fragile. Secrets and lies jeopardize trust and can damage us and our relationships, sometimes irreparably.

In 2012, I started middle school at Basis DC PCS. It was in the center of Downtown DC. Full of pedestrians walking in the street and slow cab drivers. The main reason I chose this school was because my friend was going. Before attending, we took comprehension assessments for the school. Starting sixth grade was good. I liked the school. It wasn't anything like Arts and

Technology. This school was more academic rather than creative. It was a drastic change, but I liked the school. I had an opportunity to leave that school because I was accepted at another one, where I was on the waiting list. I decided to stay, but here is the reason. The school had a personal cook. We received fresh food for lunch, but that ended, and we were back eating the nasty warmed-up lunch. The school lunch went from country club entrees to prison slop.

As the school year went on, there was one class I struggled in: Chemistry. Who would have thought that a sixth grader would be taking chemistry? Keep this in mind, I had no prior knowledge. At Arts and Technology, we learned math, reading, and social studies, which combined science and history. I was having trouble in the class and my grade started falling.

At Basis DC, we had a tracker called a communication journal. This journal was like a detailed calendar planner. In this journal, we wrote our homework and due dates. The journal helped us stay organized. I struggled and got lazy, and this is where my lying spree started.

One school day, I came home, and my mother asked if I had any homework. I lied and said I didn't have any homework. I played my game and did everything I wanted to do. I ate dinner, washed up, and went to bed. Close to three in the morning, God woke my mother up and told her to look in my bookbag. She looked in my communication journal and saw that I had homework. She woke me up and put me at the kitchen table to do my homework. Remember, this was early in the morning, and I still had to go to school that day.

In chemistry, my grade went below fifty percent, which is an F. When our teachers wanted to send a grade home, they would print the grade on a sticker and our parents had to sign it. I thought I was slick. I would take the sticker off and roll it in my pencil case. I wrote the grade I wanted in the communication journal and put a signature line under it. I went home and showed my mom. She was happy about the grade and signed the journal. When I went to school, I unrolled the sticker and placed it in my journal. So, when the teacher came to check the signature, they saw the sticker and the signature under it. I just deceived my mother. This is something I never thought I would do. But it felt good because I got away. This went on for some time following the same process. I thought I was getting away. But my days were numbered.

We had an exam, and I received a thirty-three percent. This was the lowest grade I have ever received in that class. It was a multiple-choice test that was taken on a scantron sheet. For your information, a scantron sheet, also known as a bubble sheet, is a specialized answer sheet for multiple-choice exams and surveys. They would put the sheets in the machine, and it would print the grading on the sheet. When I did not know what to do, I was disappointed but began to think of a plan. We received our sticker to put in the journal and I had my regular routine ready. But I needed proof. I wanted to show my mom tangible proof. I looked around the classroom and I got an idea from my flesh. Steal a scantron sheet. I went around the classroom and found a sheet with a ninety-two percent grade, which was excellent. I erased my classmate's name to the best of my ability and placed mine. I hid it in my notebook. A few moments later, my classmate was asking around about her sheet because it was missing. And I just sat there and said nothing. That was diabolical of me.

    I went home knowing on the inside that I was getting ready to tell a lie. I showed my mother the writing in the journal and took out the scantron. I showed her and she was proud of me. I was excited because I just got away. Later that night, I was in the tub washing myself. My mother came into the bathroom with the scantron and held it to the light. She said, "It looks like there was another name on here. Is there anything you need to tell me?" The question I always dreaded. See, my mother would ask this question every time I did something bad that she did not know. I guess it was between the Holy Spirit and her mother senses. It seems like she always knew when I did something. Quickly, I replied, "No." She brushed it off and walked out. The next day, I went to school, unrolled the sticker, placed it in the journal, and showed my teacher the signature. I was in the clear, but not for long.

A couple of days later, my teacher emailed my mother. She informed my mother that my grades were failing, and she wanted an in-person meeting. After my mom told me this, I knew this scheme was over. We traveled up to the sixth floor to my chemistry class. During the meeting, my teacher explained how my grade was steadily declining, which was different from what I was telling my mother. She told my mother that she sent the stickers home for us to show our parents, but my mother never saw the stickers. After the meeting, I knew I was done for. My first period was in the next classroom and my mother just wished me a good day.

After reminiscing this story with my mother, she revealed that she was hurt by my actions because she never expected me to do that. I wanted that day to go slow because I knew I was about to get it. School was over and I waited for her to pull up. I got in the car, and she started talking to me in a calm tone. That scared me even worse. When we got home, I got the whupping of a lifetime. The most hurtful thing wasn't the whupping. It was when my mother told me, "I can't trust you anymore." That was a hurtful feeling for both of us. From that experience, I asked my teacher for help and attended her student hours after school. By the end of the year, I raised my grade from an F to a C. I showed my mother everything, even if the grade was bad. I just wanted to regain my mother's trust.

This taught me the importance of the truth. I lied because I was lazy. I lied to avoid punishment. I lied thinking it would make my mother happy. But lies only last for a moment. While the harm done by lies can linger, dishonesty tends to expose itself. Lies self-destruct and destroy those who make them. Truth endures because there is nothing deceptive or false about it. This experience happened right before I started preaching, which made me appreciate the truth in God's word more. I told the truth no matter what. I made a promise to God, that I would never lie to His people. Never to people that trust me, even if the truth hurts. Remember, the truth will set you free. Not free from consequences, but free in your mind.

NINE

PUSHED TO COOK

"Anyone Can Cook"- Disney's Ratatouille

Every cook loves to eat. At least I do. When I was young, I enjoyed eating. I picked up a few pounds over the years. My favorite place to eat was Old Country Buffet in Forestville, Maryland. They had different prices depending on your age. I know I was twelve years old for about 3 years. The buffet had pizza, mac and cheese, fried chicken, and yeast rolls. I love yeast rolls. There was even a soft-serve ice cream machine and desserts. The food was so good that I would keep getting plates. One day, my mother, for some reason, decided to tell me that overeating is a sin. When I heard this, I was shaken. Do you mean to tell me that every plate I had when I was full was a sin?

I stopped overeating immediately. Now that I have grown up, I realize that overdoing anything is a form of gluttony.

Cooking is not just an ordinary chore or a hobby; it is an essential life skill that offers numerous benefits. From improving overall health and nutrition to fostering creativity and bringing people together, the importance of cooking cannot be overstated. I love cooking, but here is a story about how I started. My grandmother cooked every Sunday. She would either cook fried chicken, fried pork chops, or spaghetti. My grandmother is not a cook, at least not since I started cooking. But she is not the reason why I started cooking.

Around age fourteen, my mother was diagnosed with Type 2 Diabetes. Due to this, she was mostly tried because she did not have a grasp on it yet. So, it would go up and down depending on the day. This was new for me. So, I stepped up. The first meal I made was Fried Chicken and Cream Corn. To be honest, I thought I was doing something, but the chicken was a little raw. But I kept trying. At least I was at the age where I did things for myself. I knew how to resort to my beef ramen noodles. The next time I fried chicken, I did well. It was not perfect, but it was edible. But the chicken did not stay crispy long after leaving the grease. I needed to perfect my craft. The more I kept practicing, the better I got.

Soon, I started looking at cooking videos on YouTube. My favorite cooking shows were *Gordan Ramsey's Kitchen Nightmares*, *MasterChef*, and *Hell's Kitchen*. Even to this day, I have a MasterChef knife set that I use. Also, I looked at a lot of home cooks that did cooking vlogs. I found some methods on YouTube and used them when I cooked. But my mother did not like it when I experimented with the food she bought unless it came out good. One time, I tried to make homemade chicken noodle soup. I made chicken, vegetables, and noodles. I used a low-sodium store-bought chicken stock. When I mixed everything, it smelled delicious. I grabbed a spoon to taste it. Immediately, I got a headache, and it was disgusting. I told my mother, threw the mess out, and vowed to never make it again.

Some years later, I started baking cakes. That was a whole different process. For me, baking cakes is a science, whether homemade or from the box. A lot of people look down on box cake mix, but I prefer to work smarter, not harder. You can always "doctor up" your food. For your information, "doctor up" is making something that regular and perfecting it from its imperfections. Instead of using water in the cake mix, I'll use whole milk. You make the best out of what you have.

The first cake I made was a yellow cake with chocolate icing. My uncle made this cake for Thanksgiving and

Christmas. I did not want to wait for that. So, why not make it myself? I bought some cake mix and icing. But I was rushing. While the cake was in the oven, it smelled good and rose in the pan. I took it out because I thought it was done. I put the cake pan on the stove to cool down and went to do something. A few moments later, I came back to the kitchen and the middle of the cake dropped in the middle. Quickly, I put it back in the oven to finish. Since then, I learned to use a toothpick and check if the batter is cooked. I went from single-layer cakes to multi-layer cakes. I even sold some layered cakes and cupcakes.

My cooking journey was unexpected, but I love cooking for the ones I love. I dream of being married with a big family. With that dream, I think that is the reason I cook a lot of food. Over the years, I've gotten better at cooking and cook every week.

Channel Your Inner Chef! This process may take weeks, months, or even years. It truly depends on how much you want to commit to growing your list at any given time. For me, it took some time to follow recipes in videos before I felt as though I could challenge myself. You can still follow the recipe to a tee, but this is the stage where you'll want to push yourself a little further and experiment. Branching out begins with minor changes, like substituting ingredients or adding in your favorite spices. While this phase of your cooking journey may seem scary, hopefully, you feel excited, too.

The more time you spend in the kitchen, gathering information about what you like and don't like, the more you'll enjoy cooking. Soon you'll know what to stock up on and what isn't worth your money. You'll discover what you want to make from scratch and what is worth buying at the store.

There's no way to know for sure what your cooking journey will look like, though I can guarantee you will surprise yourself! I sure did. I didn't know that my mother's diagnosis would introduce me to this essential tool for life. Even though I'm far from declaring myself a chef, I feel empowered by what I've learned in the kitchen. I take pride in creating meals. Cooking is an act of self-care and an act of love. I am grateful that I can cook food for myself and others, and that is amazing.

TEN

MINISTRY:
PLEASURES AND MISERIES

"Though the Lord gives you the bread of adversity and the water of affliction, yet your Teacher will no longer hide Himself, but your eyes will [constantly] see your Teacher." – Isaiah 30:20

Have you heard the saying, "You see my glory but don't know my story?" Ministry is not for the weak and faint-hearted. But, if you focus on God, he will build you into a mighty, strong warrior. Everyone sees the lights and glory of ministry. The platforms, opportunities, and exposure. In this age, most people desire ministry for the wrong reasons. Ministry is not an occupation with money, fame, and glory. It is a lifestyle because your ministry is more creditable by the life you live. It does not matter how many scriptures you know. The word of

God must be our guiding light. Not just something that we read. As I mentioned in a previous chapter, I began my public ministry in 2013. After preaching my first sermon, "Fatih in the Fire", most of my ministry included platform services. Platform services were set apart services where multiple preachers would normally preach on a theme or topic. Some platform services did allow people to just expound on the word of God freely. Mostly, I did Last Saying of Jesus Christ or youth services. In addition, I had the opportunity to teach children's bible study. I enjoyed it even though it did not last long.

Let me tell you a quick story. One time before the bible study, my mother and I stopped at Target. Around that time, our local Target had a small food court. I went to get a personal pizza from the stand. The cashier asked me, "What church do you go to?" I told him the church and address. Can you believe I knew the address by heart? He gave me a free medium soda with my pizza. I was surprised and happy. I got something for free. But I wondered why he asked that question. I went to the car and proceeded to the church. I looked in the passenger mirror and realized something. I forgot that I had on a hat. The hat said, "Walk with Jesus, Exercise your Faith." He saw the hat.

Representing God got me blessed. Did you know that representing God sends His favor on your life? Can I encourage you? When we represent Christ in us, it's essential that God lives inside of us, wanting to radiate out from our words, thoughts, attitudes, and actions, and how we love others as He loves us. God wants to empower us as we talk, live, and think. He desires His Word to flow out of our mouths into this sin-sickened world desperately in need of spiritual healing!

As time went by, I received another opportunity to preach on a Sunday morning. I preached "Spiritual Wickedness in High Position." I didn't know that in a month, God would lead me to another ministry. Imagine a 15-year-old leaving his mother to follow God. I left my mother to follow God in the ministry he called me to. But it wasn't long after that God told her to be there for me.

At the ministry that God sent me to I served as the keyboard player. Months before the ministry started, my mother and I traveled across the DMV with the pastor to their preaching engagements. I was attending this ministry months before I joined. I joined this ministry in August 2017 during bible study. I remember coming home and I told my mom. Tears welled up in her eyes because I was leaving her. But I believe this was the initial moment where I obeyed God without parental guidance.

I just trusted God.

The pastor knew me and acknowledged the anointing on my life. They allowed me to preach one Sunday. I appreciated this moment because not every pastor is willing to allow a 15-year-old to preach to the church. Some look at age but I learned that God is timeless. He has no respect of persons. There is no age limit in experiencing God and being used by His power. The word that God gave me was "When God Places You on Hold, Don't Hang Up." Even though I never shared this, that sermon was personal for me because I felt like I was on hold concerning my ministry. I felt like I was being held back from doing the work of God that people knew I should've been doing. I felt like I should have been further in ministry than I was. But little did I know that God would make the wait worth it.

After I joined, I continued to play the keyboard. In November 2017, I was licensed as a minister and was the youngest minister. My mother bought me a black and red robe. This was my first robe of many. After this, I preached more frequently. In the next year, I received a couple of engagements to preach at other churches. I even had the opportunity to preach in Delaware. That was a good experience, but I think I could have done better. Every preacher experiences the thought and concern if their ministering isn't enough. Two years ago, I preached on Palm Sunday. The Spirit of God was dwelling with us and praise was lifted. A rhema word came out of my mouth, "Jesus is passing by and He's asking what do you want Me to do?" But I retreated to the sermon I prepared. I don't know the reason, but I did it. After church, people came to me and thanked me for the word because they needed it. Sometime later, God brought me back to that moment. He explained that He brought a "right now" word from my mouth, but my trust was in the sermon I prepared rather than trusting God Himself. Even though the sermon was good, it wasn't what God wanted to say that day. Ever since then, I have been careful in ministering God's word by giving Him the space to speak through me.

I continued to serve in the church, and I got an opportunity to preside over a Sunday morning service. I was excited because I've watched my mother do it for years. For this service, God told me, "Have a testimony service." I said, "Yes Lord", but my mistake was running my mouth to others. I went to one of the other ministers and mentioned what God told me to do. They opposed saying that the pastor does not like testimony services, which I believe was not true. I was discouraged and didn't want to preside anymore. When Sunday came, I still did not want to do it. I began to cry because I knew what God told me to do but I heard that the pastor did not approve of that. After I got myself together, I gave the offer to people to give a testimony. Some people got up and shared awesome testimonies and I felt better. Later I mentioned this to the pastor, and he encouraged me to always follow God.

In 2019, my pastor allowed me to teach bible study on the book of Revelation for some months, which was an awesome experience. A lot of people didn't come but I loved the little bit that came. I prepared worksheets and homework because I wanted the people of God to learn. Even in our last session, I showed my appreciation by giving cupcakes and certificates to everyone who attended.

In October 2019, I was consecrated as a prophet, which was an empowering moment for me. This calling was prophesied over my life for many years. I learned to embrace the prophetic ministry that God gave me. I had to realize that God would use me differently from others. One service, I was preaching, and the Holy Spirit moved me to lay hands. But little did I know what God was putting me into. Through the guidance of the Holy Spirit, I prophesied and spoke a word to every single person in the building. Every time I walked to another person, I didn't know what to tell them, but the Spirit of God knew what each person needed. Also, I learned how to back up with a person who wasn't ready to receive. One Sunday, the Spirit of God led me to lay hands and speak a word to certain people. This particular person had a wall up in the spirit and God told me to immediately back away. You might say that I could have still spoken it, but I would have. But the Lord taught me that day how to be sober in my gift. We had power-packed services, where the power of God was so overwhelming that we couldn't leave immediately. We just basked in the glory of God.

Now, this is a sensitive part of my ministry story. Every moment of ministry is not perfect. I will never claim that we are perfect people, but there is a standard of righteousness we must represent as Christ Redeemed Believers. God uses these moments to teach us more about others and, most importantly, ourselves. As time passed, some things in our ministry took a turn. In my view, the pastor's character started to change based on the people who were appeasing his commands. There was a group of people who catered to him and were ready to bounce and oppose anyone who didn't "dance to the music." The real test of my integrity started in 2020. There were moments where I stood in the pulpit and opposition was coming from the pews and the pulpit. There were multiple times when I cried out to God asking why I was treated like this. I didn't disrespect anybody and didn't say much. I became stagnant in my gift. I wouldn't speak what God said because I developed a fear of the people. I was encouraged to speak what God said but when they didn't like it, it was a problem. The devil didn't put a muzzle on my mouth because I did it myself.

Everyone remembers how 2020 started with the pandemic of Covid 19. Churches were closing their doors for the safety of their members. The world, as we knew it, changed. Our church was closed for a few Sundays, but we returned. Some months later, I realized that I had not been allowed to preside over a service in two years. I expressed my concern to the head of the ministerial staff, and they said they would put it on the list. When the list came out, I was not on it.

The next month, we had a ministerial meeting. Normally, I wouldn't say anything. But this time, I publicly communicated my concern. In front of everyone, the head of the ministerial staff proclaimed that I should have come to them, even though we had the conservation two weeks before. They claimed that they did not think I could do it based on what happened the first time. I responded with this, "If you trust me to stand in that pulpit and preach God's word, how can you not trust me to preside? After this comment, they proceeded to talk and said that God should have told me to call them. I was enraged and yelled, "You're not going to bring God into this!" The minister on the pew in front of me stood up, turned around, and waved his finger in my face. He said that I should have talked to the head minister if I had a problem, which is something I already did. While this was going on, the pastor was sitting in the back agreeing with everyone else. At that moment, the devil told me these words: "Knock all of them out. I'll give you the strength." Let me tell you something. The devil will give you the power to do his will. I began to cry because the Spirit of wisdom played out the situation if I had obeyed the devil. I saw what I would lose. I looked over at my mother, who was furious, and told her I wanted to go. As I was walking out, I glanced at the pastor. Even though my eyes were filled with tears, the pastor's face was so dark and disapproving. We were outside and a couple of minutes later the pastor came out. In my mind, I was like, "Why are you here?" He came trying to tell me that he'd handle it and if I had any problems, just come to him. But I couldn't receive that because I was so hurt. Two days later, I connected with the drummer and told him I was not playing the keyboard until further notice. In my hurt, God showed me one of our other keyboard players. This guy was being raised in the faith and was a consistent member. When I saw his face, it was a way of God telling me, "Don't give up for him." Immediately,

I texted the drummer back and disregarded the message.

The next Sunday, my mother and I still went to church. Hatred filled my heart. I didn't want to speak or look at the people. The pastor was preaching, and he started talking about being in error. And for some reason, he pointed in my direction during one of his statements. I didn't know whether it was intentional or not. The devil whispered in my ear, "Pick up that keyboard and knock them all out." But again, the Spirit of Wisdom showed me the result of the act I resisted. But I was still mad. For the next couple of months, every other minister preached their opinions while throwing daggers at me. I was on the schedule to preach on the last Sunday of that year. While preparing my sermon, I wrote a whole section throwing the daggers back at them. But God stopped me and told me to delete it. I cried out to God because I couldn't take it anymore. I couldn't take the ridicule and lies. David had two opportunities to kill King Saul. In similarity, I had many times when I could have done something, but I would have aborted God's plan for my life. There were even times I wanted to leave the church, but it wasn't God's timing. When I preached, the message that God gave me was "My Goal is to make in the Kingdom." My focus was not on the people, but it was on God.

In 2022, God was dealing with me in a mighty way. January

was a month of power for me. On January 1, 2022, I received a word from God, and I wrote it down on my computer. The Lord said, "This is the year of the Overcomer. For standing in the face of adversity, for standing in the face of tribulation, for standing in the face of death, I shall reward thee in this season. For I have stored up your faithfulness, I have stored up your tears. Behold, there is an outpour being released on those who have overcome." He took me to Galatians 6:9, "Let us not be weary in well doing: for in due season, we shall reap, if we faint not." This message blessed me because I was going through a personal struggle in prayer. It got to the point that anytime I prayed in the church, something was choking me. One Sunday evening, we had a service, and they asked me to pray. As I began praying, I felt my throat closing rapidly, but I pressed through the boundaries of my flesh. Afterward, I felt like I couldn't breathe, and the saint prayed for my restoration. I fasted and prayed for my strength. I questioned myself: How can you preach God's word and be scared to pray? I told God I wanted power over this issue, and I told the devil to give me my voice back. On January 15, 2022, the Lord came back and said, "There is victory in your mouth." The reason why demonic forces try to attack our breathing is because our breakthrough is in our mouth. Our mouth is powerful according to the word of God. The bible declares that whatsoever we bind on earth, shall be bound in heaven. And whatsoever we loose on earth, shall be loosed in heaven. Ever since then, God planted my feet firmer. To this day, I can pray without any hindrance because God gave me the power to defeat the enemy. That year, I preached more than I ever did and every time there was a fresh word from God.

Later that year, I had a divine experience with God. In February, my mother preached during Sunday worship. After God used her to minister and lay hands, God told me to pray for her. I got off the keyboard and went to the pulpit to pray. After I finished, I felt these sharp pains in the sides of my abdomen. The pain was not as painful as medical specialists would consider, but it was a birthing pain. How do I know that? I don't know. This was the first time I travailed in the Spirit. Travailing in the Spirit is a type of prayer that is considered one of the most powerful forms of prayer. The bibles speak about how the Spirit of God intercedes for us through wordless groans. When the Holy Spirit travails through you, you may experience groaning. At other times, it may be an ongoing burden deep in your spirit that you continue to pray for. I started birthing a prophetic word before I spoke it. It kept moving from side to side because it was a living and active word from God.

When I looked at the video, my voice sounded different because I was prophesying from another realm. I look back at the experience and realize that God was equipping me. To this day, whenever God is equipping me in the Spirit, I feel the birthing pains all over again. When it comes, I just give God another "yes" for what He's equipping me for.

On November 6, 2022, I preached a message called "It's All Good." I did not know that it was my last time ministering there. I reached a point where the opposition eased but my time of departure was drawing near. I sought God and he said, "It's time to go." When I asked God to change me, He gave me direction. Now, I still had resentment in me, and I believe in writing a resignation letter. I wrote a professional "nice nasty" letter. The letter was so cutthroat that the people who read it felt bad and it wasn't geared towards them. Trust me, I have a way with words. But the Lord corrected me, and I changed the letter. I explained how grateful I was for the good times and let God handle the rest.

My mother and I peacefully departed the ministry, we spoke with the pastor, returned our licenses per his request, and said goodbye to all the members present. I didn't know where God would lead me, but I made a vow that I would follow Him. I still loved the ministry, but there were some things in me that

God needed to develop and change. I'll talk about that later.

Ministry is my life, not my role. This is one thing that I can't see myself not doing. I strive to be an example to many. I praise God for the pleasures and miseries of ministry because it shaped my perception of God. We don't always understand God. We don't always know what God is up to. And sometimes, we struggle with that because, as His children, there are times when we question what it is that He's doing. But I've learned that God never asked us to understand Him. He never asked us to know what He's doing. Let's take a cake for example. A cake with frosting looks delicious as it sits whole on a kitchen table. Everyone wants a piece of it. It looks appealing. It smells appealing. But no one saw the process it took to become a whole cake except the baker. The baker is the master of the entire process. This was my making process. I can stand confident in God because he mixed all the pleasures and miseries and made a masterpiece. The masterpiece is not me because I am far from perfection. But the masterpiece is the testimony of a sovereign God.

ELEVEN

OFF TO COLLEGE

"Trust in the Lord with all thine heart; and lean not unto thine own understanding. In all thy ways acknowledge him, and he shall direct thy paths" – Proverbs 3:5-6

I am a first-generation college student on my mother's family side. This journey was great but there were still some struggles. I did not have anyone to tell me what to expect or what to prepare for. At times, I wished someone told me the process that came with the product. I received words of prophecy, encouragement, and guidance from many, including my pastor, of my success in college. But I learned that God is more concerned about the process rather than the product. My experience was a journey of faith while leaning on God every step of the way.

Allow me to pivot for a moment. I want to tell you a story. During our upper school years, we were allowed to leave the school for lunch. We signed out and went to the restaurants near the school. I went to the McDonalds two blocks from the school. Most of the time, I walked by myself. I wasn't scared but I was attentive. There was a certain homeless guy outside the McDonalds. His hair was wild, and he wore a gray sweatsuit. I saw him occasionally and sometimes he asked for change. One day, God told me to give this man a dollar. The next day, I went to McDonalds, but he wasn't there. I didn't see him for a week and got concerned. Now, I could have spread the dollar and didn't worry. But I kept bringing the dollar to school just in case I saw him again. One day, my friend offered to walk with me to McDonalds. When we arrived, I still didn't see the guy. We went inside and ordered our food. When I came back out, he was sitting by the tree outside. I went to him and gave him the dollar in front of my friend. I walked away with joy and happiness because I obeyed God. After that day, I never saw the man again. I don't know if he was an angel or if God just placed him there for that moment. Now, back to the story.

In 2018, my high school assigned us to college counseling classes, which happened every other day. I was assigned to one of the counselors, who happened to be my earlier English teacher and academic advisor. The class was very educational and helped me in deciding on what colleges I wanted to attend. At first, I wanted to attend Howard University. If you were to ask me why, I still can't tell you to this day. Plus, my mom didn't want to go anyway. I would have been miserable with them DC rats. But back to the story.

I don't know how Bowie State University became my first choice. I loved how the campus looked on the websites and the arts programs. But I don't know how that became my decision. In December of 2018, I went on a campus tour and fell in love with the campus building, especially the Fine and Performing Arts Center. Plus, they served soul food and fried chicken every Wednesday. So, that was a win for me. But I still struggled during the wait.

At church, everyone was excited for me. Some people were urging me to go far and leave my mother. But my heart and spirit said "Stay close" because I just started building my ministry and was not comfortable being far away. On Friday, October 19, 2018, Prophetess Ward, who was in a prayer group with my mother, decided to take out my mom for her birthday. When I heard that her mother, Apostle Frances Brown, was coming, I told my mom I was not going to school, and I was going with her. Around that time, I was struggling to find a college to go to but still considering Bowie State University. Even though we were there to celebrate my mom, the conversation was about me. And Apostle Brown confirmed where my heart and spirit were. She told me, " You cannot go far because you have a ministry here." That was the confirmation I needed.

I want to pause and talk about faith. Can we be honest, sometimes we do not feel it. We feel discouraged because we have not seen results. Or maybe the results have gotten worse. We feel frustrated with God's timing because people are being blessed and receiving promises, but there's nothing in our hands. Going into 2019, I started to hear my classmates get accepted into colleges, even their first choice. By this time, I've submitted my application to Bowie State University. But I was afraid of something. My Grade Point Average, commonly known as the dreaded GPA. My GPA coming out of high school, at the time, was 2.15. That's not bad, but it's not good either. If you want it as a letter grade, it was between a C and C+.

Knowing this concern, my college counselor worked hard with me to achieve this goal. One day, she asked me to find the contact information of Bowie State's head of admissions. I found the contact information during the class and gave it to her. A couple of days later, she informed me that she contacted Bowie State's head of admissions and set up a potential meeting with him. I don't know what other college counselors would go through such a length to help me. In an email, she wrote these exact words to my mother: "Dear Ms. Brown, I had a lovely conversation with the head of admission. I told him that, to really judge what Davon has to offer, one needs to meet him and get to know him in person, rather than simply on paper." How sweet was that?

On February 18, 2019, I met the head of admissions. He took my mother and I into his office and began to talk. Let's be honest. I was terrified because I was meeting with the person who had human power over my acceptance. Plus, I'm an introvert. I introduced myself and told him about my experiences in high school and life. I mentioned that I was a youth minister and loved God. As he talked, he mentioned things about him, such as his upbringing, his academic struggles, and his religion. You wouldn't have thought he was Muslim. But he could relate to me. He gave me some instructions: Raise my GPA to 2.3 and get a joint score of 1000 for my highest Math and English SAT. The next day, I checked my college board account, and behold, I already had a joint score of 1010. So, half of the work was done.

Months later, I still didn't hear anything. After the work I've put in, the prayers I've prayed, and the praises I've given, I still felt hopeless. I told my college counselor, "If I don't get into Bowie State, I'm going to a bible seminary school and getting a job."

One Saturday, my mother and I went out to the store. I had a huge headache that day. When we came home, my grandmother told me that I had mail. I looked at the table and saw a small white envelope. If anybody knows anything about college acceptance letters, the regular white envelope means you're not accepted. If you are accepted, you'll receive a big envelope package with your acceptance letter. My mother went to the bathroom and started praying. I just knew that Bowie State rejected me. I opened the envelope, and it was only a letter from the finance office. I was so relieved but still waiting.

I became discouraged, despite hearing the good news that was promised to me by God. One night around 12:30 am, I had a personal conversation with God. I expressed how discouraged I was during the process. And in my sadness and confusion, I had a Jesus moment as if I were in the garden of Gethsemane. Out of my spirit, I said this phrase, "God, you make the best decisions, and I trust you."

Later that week, I received an email from the financial

office that I'd been accepted. I was in shock and couldn't process it. Have you ever waited for something so long that when it falls in your hands, you can't process it immediately? I called my mother, while she was at work, and told her, "I think I got accepted." She told me to send her the email. She called back excitedly. My mother showed her co-worker, and she started crying. So, both of them are crying and I'm still in shock. I felt a spirit of relief because my waiting paid off. A few days later, I received that big envelope package with my acceptance letter and documents for my next steps.

In June 2019, I attended the new student orientation (NSO) at BSU. I had to stay on campus overnight. I packed my luggage and belongings for the day. On the arrival day, I went to the registration at the student center. This was a new experience for me. The NSO staff were current students, and they were wild. Not my cup of tea. I prefer mild and mellow people, not wild and partying. After all of the chants and yelling, we had lunch in the dining hall. I met two other guys that were there. Later we had the chance to go to our dorms. The dorm that they put us in was "Towers." Towers is normally a female dormitory at Bowie State. For NSO, they put all of us there. Later that night, they wanted to have a party for the incoming freshmen. The party was too much for me and some people agreed. The party was behind a stage curtain, and we just went and sat in the audience while the others twerked and danced behind the curtains. Soon, an adult came and asked if we wanted to leave, which was the best question I've been asked all day. I went back to my dorm and went to sleep. The next day was more academic. We took pictures to receive our Bulldog IDs and registered for classes. This was a productive day. Then, we had lunch that our families could come to. My mother and grandmother came for me but by this time I was ready to go home.

My first semester began in August and my mother and grandmother helped me move in. For all of my college years, my mother and grandmother were the only ones that helped me move in and out. I am grateful for them. I was naturally ready for college. I can't say that I was worried, but my transition was graceful. I did have anxiety or worry about schooling. I was concerned about my mother though. We've never been apart in that magnitude. Back then, she had these breathing episodes where she would start choking at night and I was always there to help her. I put her in God's hand while I was away. I was grateful to be making history in my family.

I had a two-hour math class every day at eight in the morning. Imagine just waking up and the first thing to do is look at a screen for two hours. I remember one day I overslept. My mother was calling my phone repeatedly. I woke up 10 minutes before class started. I got up, wiped my face, put on my clothes, and ran out of the dorm. My face was ashy, and my clothes were not straight. I made it to class because the math and science building was next to my dormitory. But I realized something, I left my phone. So, my mother is worried about me and can't get to me. But God told her that I was alright. After class, I went back to my dorm to properly get myself together and called my mom.

I enjoyed English 101. I was surprised that many other students didn't know what a thesis statement was. I learned that at Basis DC. After all the essays we did, I couldn't forget was a thesis statement was. I wrote my first college essay and received an A+. That semester was awesome, I had great professors. At the end of the semester, I went to the grade's portal, and I was excited. I received a 3.8 GPA. This previous high school with a 2.3 GPA received a 3.8 GPA in one semester.

As time went by, I stayed on the dean's list with exceptional grades. Of course, I had some classes that were a struggle, but I came out on top. Even during the pandemic, my grades didn't decrease, and I was excelling. During my years at Bowie State

University, I have juggled school, family, ministry, and life in general. In December 2023, I graduated with a Bachelor of Science in Visual Communication and Digital Media Arts. Also, I graduated with magna cum laude honors with a 3.7 GPA. I thank my professors and friends in the Department of Fine and Performing Arts at Bowie State University for making this experience worth it. I left BSU with a higher consciousness and a wider perception of my opportunities in the world.

TWELVE

THANK YOU

"Bear with each other and forgive one another if any of you has a grievance against someone. Forgive as the Lord forgave you." - Colossians 3:13

Have you heard the phrase, "Forgiveness is not for the other person, it is for you!" Sometimes, I believe we hear and pass down this phrase but never understand its depth. I truly believe that forgiveness is healing. That forgiveness is redemption. That forgiveness lifts and settles your spirit, whether you're giving or receiving. I think there's something wonderful about letting go of the pain in this way— knowing that someone has given you a second chance or deciding after you've been broken to accept someone's apology and set both of your hearts free. I even learned that I still could forgive without apologies. That's what Christ did for us. He forgave us without an apology. He forgave us because we didn't know how to apologize or what to apologize for since we were ignorant of who He was.

From my experience, forgiveness has changed my life. Accepting apologies from people who have discouraged me, forgiving people even when they haven't asked for it, and letting go—this has healed my heart in ways I could have never imagined. But this wasn't easy. And not all stories are the same. Sometimes forgiving people is hard. Sometimes it hurts too much. Forgiveness doesn't mean you're obligated to stay in a relationship or marriage with someone who has destroyed the foundation of everything you've built. Forgiveness doesn't mean you keep a close friendship with the person who betrayed you. Forgiveness doesn't mean you continue to engage with family members who have proven their disloyalty, time and time again. Forgiveness means you accept what wrongs have been done to you, you let go of those wrongs, you calm your heart with God's love and patience, and you begin again—with or without that person, it's up to you. But I still think there's power in forgiving because it helps to free yourself from what's been trapping you and holding you down. It's a reminder of God's love and faithfulness when you treat others with kindness, even when they don't deserve it. And it helps you just as much, if not more when you free your heart from that bitterness and pain.

For years, I heard my mother say, "One day, I'm going to call your father and tell him thank you." After a couple of years, I took it as a joke because she would bring it up occasionally. Well, that day came. Out of nowhere, she said that she was going to call him. She did not have his number, so she messaged his oldest son through Facebook. Before this, I thought I forgave my father. It's easy to think you forgave a person when they are not in your presence. Remember in the earlier chapter, he became non-existent in my mind. I even blocked him from my Facebook page. Later that day, we went to the laundry mat. He called her phone. She answered the phone and began to talk to him. I didn't feel anything while she was talking. We went to the car and the phone ended up connecting to the car. The moment I heard his voice, all the emotion tied to him came up. Emotions and memories that I haven't felt in a while. My body was still, and I could not talk until he was off the phone. While on the phone, he proposed seeing us the next week since he visited his mother on weekends. I didn't reject the offer because I thought that was the Christian thing to do. I'm a preacher and I preach the message of forgiveness and reconciliation. But it felt different when God came down my street.

That entire week, I was in my dorm talking everything out. I was angry. I was sad. I was bitter. All these emotions had a counseling session with God that week. On that day, I was nervous about seeing him. I haven't seen him in a couple of years. We decided to eat at Outback Steakhouse, but he was coming to pick us up. What a bummer! Not only do I have to see you, but I must ride in the same car. Let alone in the front seat next to him. When I couldn't do anything else, I talked to my Heavenly Father and asked Him for strength. When he pulled up, God put a smile on my face that I didn't even feel. My mother said that I was smiling, but I didn't feel like it or wanted to. At the dinner, there was a lot of small talk. When I say small, I mean tiny talk because I didn't have any type of conversation in me. All I did was answer questions. My mother just talked to him. We hit a point where he wanted to give us his number. When he called my phone his number was already there. Was that embarrassing? Not for me, but for him. After that night, I believe it was the start of my healing process.

Another time, He decided to take me bowling. Bowling is something that we have in common. He used to take my little brothers and me bowling sometimes. We had a fun time, and I began to open up a little. After bowling, we went to eat something. While we were there, we began to talk about some things that happened in the past. It was a good conversation. When we got back in the car, we talked a little more, but it took a turn for me. He mentioned me unfriending him on Facebook. Immediately, I retreated in my mind. Why is he still concerned about Facebook, and I am right here? I got out of the car and went into the house.

We didn't interact for a couple of months after that. Every time he wanted to do something, I was either running errands or going to church. There were times when I didn't respond to his texts. About a year later, He tried to call me, but it went to voicemail. I was in the basement of our house and decided to text him back. Months later, my mother invited him to our house. I was unsettled. I hadn't seen him and now he's coming into our house. This time, I didn't have a week to prepare myself. It was the same day I found out. He came bearing gifts, which were food. My grandmother and niece happened to be there too. I'll admit something, I was uncomfortable at first, but I opened up. The thing that helped was us playing UNO. In result, the visit was decent. It was so decent that I texted him and thanked him for coming. I even mentioned how I felt about it. This was a huge step for me. From that point on, my father and I have been building a relationship. I am learning how to communicate with him as an adult. We have fellowshipped more together, and I had chances to fellowship with him and my mother in the same room intentionally. This is an image that I never dreamed of or desired because I threw all of that away. My father and I have a lot in common. We love to cook, our favorite color is Red, and we love vanilla ice cream.

One day, I was in the basement and began to talk to God. I told Him that I wanted to make peace. I know that I have hopes and dreams for my life, but I never know when God will call me to His throne. I would always go to God and say, "If my father wants a relationship, he needs to prove it." Then God asked me, "Do you want the relationship?" The Lord turned the question on me. I decided to give my father another chance. God said, "No matter how much he does, you'll never be satisfied because you have to want this." It opened my eyes to the truth: I couldn't ask my father to prove something that I didn't want. The Bible tells us to forgive, and we will be forgiven. Blessed is the merciful, for they will obtain mercy.

God took me as far as to make peace with my previous pastor. I didn't know if it was God telling me to make peace or if I was in my feelings. But God responded, "You know it's me because you're scared to do it." I asked God to give me the words to say. I messaged them, not knowing if they would see it. I explained how I couldn't change the past, and that God has done something in me. I thank my previous pastor for being the leader that God knew I needed for my journey. Most importantly, I told them that I loved them. They responded and we made peace. I received my healing.

In my healing process, God even showed me the places where I went wrong. Sometimes, we go through things, and we can see the wrong of everyone else. What about the wrong in us? At the time, I wasn't aware of my inward shortcomings. God revealed to me that, while in that ministry, I became a fault finder. What is a fault finder? According to what God told me, a fault finder is a person who walks into a situation looking for something to be wrong or others to mess up. He brought before me instances where I was fault finding God's people, including the pastor. I said things in private conversations and even walked into services criticizing many things that people did. Even though most of the things I said were true and most came to pass, God said that it wasn't my place. In forgiveness, God will show you where you must grow.

This healing taught me how to give up my right to be right for peace's sake. What does that mean? It means that forgiveness is not the opportunity to prove how right you were, but rather it is a moment to embrace freedom from the past.

Romans 14:19 states, "Let us pursue the things which make for peace and the things by which one may edify another." We waste so much time trying to prove our side of the story, yet it's not beneficial.

Resentment can sometimes linger for years, even if we believe that we've "moved on" or "forgotten about it." To release resentment, reflect on why the person may have committed the offense, sit with the pain, and then try to forgive the other person because forgiveness can instill a sense of strength that overpowers bitterness. Forgiving someone is the best way to take back your power. But to be clear, forgiveness isn't about saying what the person did was OK. It's about choosing to let go of the hurt and anger that interferes with your ability to enjoy life. Forgiveness is not a one-time action, but it is a daily choice. I choose forgiveness every day. Memories will come back, and emotions will follow them. But the power is when you choose to forgive. Do not let anybody or anything take your power to choose. If you allow the offense to take possession of your power, it will control every fiber of your soul. Unforgiveness is like drinking poison and expecting someone else to die. How do I know that I've walked in true forgiveness? It is when I don't desire to hear anything wrong about the person. It is when the essence of that person or offense doesn't move my soul. It is when I carry an attitude like King David, who said, "It is good for me that I have been afflicted, That I may learn Your statutes."

I encourage you to embrace forgiveness because there is healing and power in it. With this power, you receive control of your thoughts and emotions. I got my power back. Now, get yours back!

THIRTEEN

MIND UNDER CONSTRUCTION

"Let this mind be in you, which was also in Christ Jesus:" – Philippians 2:5

What does under construction mean? Under construction refers to a building, structure, or project that is unfinished but actively being worked on. When something is under construction, it's not yet complete. However, it's actively being worked on, and progress is being made towards the finished product. This means that while it may not be fully functional or usable yet, it's on its way there.

This chapter is the reason why I wrote this book. It started last year (2023). The mind is the complex of faculties involved in perceiving, remembering, considering, evaluating, and deciding. The mind is, in some sense, reflected in such occurrences as sensations, perceptions, emotions, memory, desires, various types of reasoning, motives, choices, traits of personality, and the unconscious. Mind is a term that refers to the immaterial aspect of who we are that typically refers to the faculty of cognition. The Bible does not have a single word for mind but uses different terms such as heart, intellect, or understanding. This is the story of how God changed my mind.

After we transitioned from the ministry we were attending, I was fully trusting God. In January 2023, I was allowed to have an empowerment service. I sought God for a theme, and He entitled the service, "Renewing My Yes." This is the word He gave me during my departure. I had to renew my yes to God because the "yes" for that ministry had expired. In seeking God, I asked him how I should encourage his people. He said, "Tell Your Testimony." I couldn't believe that He told me to do this. It was funny because, a year before this, He told me these words: "Do not withhold your testimony because of the people involved."

The night came and I wanted to broadcast it on Facebook Live. After some concerns, I decided not to, but the Lord told me to do so. This was so strange. He told me to tell my ministry testimony and, now broadcast it. After the service, I received a phone call that the people involved were in an uproar. It wasn't because of what I said, it was Facebook Live. They believed that I shouldn't have done that. But I kept following God.

At this point, I was still in college because I had to complete an additional semester due to being misadvised. It was in my last semester, and I was finishing my senior thesis project. It was a stressful time. I prayed to God because I was ready to return to the pulpit to preach. During that time, my mother and I were fellowshipping with our local churches, but I wasn't used to not preaching publicly. Social media was alright, but it doesn't compare to preaching in person. Before I departed from the previous ministry, I preached frequently. I felt like I didn't feel God like I used to. Yet, I kept trusting God even though God had me in a still place.

On September 15, 2023, I celebrated 10 years of ministry. This was a huge milestone for me. That night, I had a dream that I had a nervous breakdown. When I woke up, I rebuked the dream and went on with my day. The next week, I was asked to minister at a church we fellowshipped with. I was excited and eagerly said yes to the assignment. I began seeking God, but He wasn't saying anything. I just brushed it off and gave it some time. As days went by, I got worried. God wasn't speaking to me like He did before. On that Saturday before I had to preach, I was irritated. I was stressed out with school, and life, and could not hear God for nothing. I wrote sermons but they didn't come together. I tried to conjure some type of message to see if He was going to start talking. Isn't that funny? When we become desperate, we will try to make something up and ask God to move according to our efforts, instead of waiting on Him. I needed my black clergy robe from my grandmother's house, but my mother's car wasn't ready from the car dealership. It seemed like everything wasn't working for me. I got so upset that I said, "I wish I never would have said yes!" My mother was so upset at my outburst that she went upstairs to her room.

I sat at the kitchen table, and I felt like I was losing my mind. For your information, I was not contemplating suicide, but I just knew I was going to be admitted somewhere. I was there for five hours wondering in my mind. I was fighting the devil in my flesh. Small tears were falling like a broken faucet. The devil told me, "I'm taking your mind tonight, and you're going to lose it and you're going to be in the hospital when you're supposed to be preaching." My niece was with us, and she kept coming to the table. I tried to hide it from her, but on the inside, I was fighting in my mind.

Soon, my mother came down and asked me a question. "Didn't you ask for this?" It was a reality check. I asked God for this. But in a moment, I had a mental breakdown. I started rocking back and forth, exuding this sound of frustration. I was sweating and crying. But my mother prayed for me, and my niece comforted me. After the mental breakdown, I could not think of anything. God shut down my mental faculties. The only desire He gave me that night was to wash up, eat, and go to bed. I didn't have the desire to talk. If I talked, it wasn't above a whisper. Sometimes, God gets us to our weakest point just to give us the strength we need. There is strength in a weak believer. Psalm 27:13 says, "I would have fainted, unless I had believed that I would see the goodness of the Lord in the land of the living." During the breakdown, I might have slipped but I didn't faint. Why didn't I faint? Because I still believed in God. Thank God for faith. Allow me to encourage you: Whatever you are dealing with, don't stop believing. When you slip off the cliff of your mind, God allows His word to be a hook in your soul. In our weakest, God's strength is perfected in us, and He gets the glory out of our affliction.

The next morning, which was Sunday, God woke me up around 4:30 am. Of course, I was tired, but I've waited all week to hear from God. I was not missing this moment with Him. I got my laptop and went to the kitchen table. I received a word from God in the same place where the enemy thought he had the victory. The message God gave me was "Caved In After A Victory." This message holds a special place in my heart because that is how I felt. Caved In! God explained everything that happened last night. He explained how the breakdown was for my good. He put my mind under construction. God gave me a proposal: "If you give me your mind, I'll give you my mind." If I gave up my feelings, reasoning, and understanding, He would give me His mind and His thoughts toward my life. I had to lose my mind to gain His mind.

In 1st Kings 9, God tells Elijah to Go out on the mountain. He stood there and the Lord passed by. A mighty windstorm hit the mountain, where the rocks were torn loose but the Lord was not in the wind. After the wind, there was an earthquake, But the Lord was not in the earthquake. After the earthquake, there was a fire, but the Lord was not in the fire. But after all of that noise and dynamics, here comes a still small voice. God showed Elijah where he had messed up. Elijah got so hooked on the noise that he did not seek God's voice.

Sometimes, we get so hooked on the noise of social media, opinions, reports, and past victories, that we forget to seek His voice. We get hooked on the analysis, the translation of Greek and Hebrew scriptures, the apologetics of doctrines, and we forget His voice. It was in my weakest moment that I saw more of who God is. And now that I know who God is, I know who I am. I encourage you to learn how to see yourself as God sees you. God's opinion is the one that counts. Accept what God says about you, agree with Him that it is true of you, and become the spiritual person you are. Understanding who you are in Christ will give you a strong foundation to build your life on. Knowing who you are in Jesus is the key to a successful Christian life and a life lived ON purpose. Your identity doesn't depend on something you do or have done. Your true identity is who God says you are. Once you choose to follow Jesus you become a new creation, the old you pass away, and you become who you are in Him. Find out what God says about you and agree with Him.

God brought me through a weak moment, but the glory that is before me is greater than the sting of my affliction. He had to break me to make me. For my weakness became a portal for God's strength. Allow God to renew your mind. Give up your understanding, because He never asked us to understand Him or whatever He's doing. Yet, He did command us to trust Him. When you operate in the mind of God and trust Him fully, you will have a new vision, new perspective, and new movement.

You will start moving differently. You will learn how to respond to situations as opposed to just reacting. This mind that I have, the world didn't give it to me. Because the world didn't give it, the world can't take it away. God built my mind.

CONCLUSION:
GOD BUILT ME INTO MYSELF

"Then the word of the Lord came to me, saying, O house of Israel, cannot I do with you as this potter? saith the Lord. Behold, as the clay is in the potter's hand, so are ye in mine hand, O house of Israel." –
Jeremiah 18: 5-6

God uses many images in scripture to describe His relationship with His people. He uses the image of the shepherd and sheep. He uses the image of a husband and a wife. He uses the image of a father and His children. In the image of the shepherd and sheep, He provides for us. In the image of the husband and wife, He loves us unconditionally. In the image of the father and His children, He's always watching over us. But one of the greatest images of God is the picture of the potter and the clay. We are on God's pottery wheel being molded by God. I believe that many of us question the Lord's purpose and wonder what type of vessel He is making us into. As I cannot fully see my vision until it is near completion, I do not believe we fully understand the vessel that God is molding us into until He is ready for us to know.

Clay does not have its own will and cannot turn itself into any of these things on its own. The clay does not put itself onto the potter's wheel to be molded into a cup, plate, or pot. Clay does not put itself inside of an oven to be baked into brick. For clay to serve a valuable purpose, it is necessary for a potter to have a purpose for it and to then mold it into the vessel and as he or she desires it to be.

It is the potter that goes out into the mud, finds a purpose for it, and digs the clay from the mud. The potter is the one who puts the shapeless and lifeless clay onto the spinning wheel. It is the potter who then digs his or her hands into the clay or around the clay to form it and give it its purpose. So, who is it that has the power and is sovereign here: the potter or the clay? The sovereign one in this situation – the one that has all authority and power – is the potter.

Sometimes God must use a mallet. After the clay is cleansed and processed, it is placed on a table and beaten to remove the air bubbles. If the air bubbles are not removed, when He gets it on the wheel and fastens it into the vessel, there will be weak spots. Sometimes, He must beat us to bless us, hurt us to heal us, and knock us down to pick us up.

Yes, we endure struggle and yes, we go through some things while living in this world. But I truly believe that this is what God is molding us into today. The goal is for us to one day be perfect as God is perfect and righteous. By molding us into this vessel, we become a vessel that the Lord can use in our world today to edify others as well! I will say, however, that I do believe part of the answer has already been given to us in scripture. God ultimately wants us to fully be in His image and likeness. In the lives we live, God puts on His finishing touches and will one day show off His artwork in His heavenly kingdom.

Again, I say, we cannot become those things if God does not have His work with us today. If we do not cooperate in the hands of God, how can we become such a vessel? Sometimes the Lord must wet the clay so that He can loosen it up to mold it and shape it. Sometimes God must make the clay firm so that He can mold it and shape it into the vessel He requires it to be. We may not see nor understand His purpose for us now, but one day it will become clear, and we will see His good work and God will be glorified.

When God made me, He had those same intentions for me.

God never starts a process in you without His intentions. Everything that has happened in my life has shaped me into who I am today. I was shaped to make a difference. God can take the mess in your life and bring a message out of it. He can take the test in your life and create and testimony out of it. He can take a crisis and show Christ through it. God doesn't waste any experience you have. Through writing this book, God wanted me to realize that all these experiences have shaped who I am, whether I liked it or not.

Now that you have looked in my life, you see that God will use anyone for His glory. In conclusion of this book, I commemorate the last 23 years of life back to God for His Glory. These are the many things that I was released to share with you. God has taken me to another stage in my life and ministry. I pray that my life was a blessing to you.

Remember this: God loves you enough that He takes His time building you into yourself.

Who Am I? I am Davon Tyree Brown!

ABOUT THE AUTHOR

Jeremiah 1:5 declares. "Before I formed you in the womb, I knew you [and approved of you as My chosen instrument], And before you were born, I consecrated you [to Myself as My own]; I have appointed you as a prophet to the nations."

Through the assurance of the word of God, Elder Davon Brown was born in this world on Thursday, August 16, 2001. Since his youth, he always had a passion for serving God and preaching the word of God. He was given the gift of music and started his journey in the music ministry. Davon was christened by the late Rev. Thomas Harris at Greater New Foundation Full Gospel Church under the leadership of the late Bishop Roscoe Harris Sr. Davon served as one of the church's drummers. In February of 2008, Davon followed his mother to join Gethsemane Bible

Center under the leadership of Bishop Linwood Harris and Pastor Stephanie Harris. He served as the church's drummer until God transitioned him to play the keyboard. On September 15, 2013, Elder Davon preached his first sermon, titled "Faith in The Fire," for the

Pastor's Birthday Celebration. "Faith in the Fire" was the ignition of Elder Davon Brown's ministry.

In 2015, Elder Davon founded DB Filming Services, which is currently known as Davon Brown Designs, which supplies graphic design products and services. Elder Davon is known for professionalism and quality services. On November 12, 2017, he was licensed to be a minister in the Lord's church. While continuing his journey with God, he has accomplished many academic achievements. In elementary school, he published two children's books, "A Fun Day Out" and "Davon's Memoir," through Art and Technology Academy's writing contest.

In May 2019, he received his high school diploma and graduated from Basis DC Public Charter School. In 2019, Elder Davon started college at Bowie State University. During his college years, Elder Davon participated in many projects with his class. He received an opportunity to represent Bowie State in the United States Postal Service's Direct Effect Mail Innovation Challenge.

On October 27, 2019, Elder Davon was ordained to walk into the office of a prophet and received his certification of being an ordained prophet. From that day forward, God has taken him to higher heights in the spirit as he operates in an office that God sealed on his life since birth.

In 2021, Elder Davon Brown became a Christian author by releasing a book on spiritual growth entitled, Thing on These Things. Since then, he has published two other books on Amazon, *It's Personal: Why A*

ABOUT THE AUTHOR

Relationship with God Is Important and *The Revelation of Daring Faith: Push Your Faith Beyond the Edge.*

In 2023, Elder Davon graduated from Bowie State University with a Bachelor of Science in Visual Communication and Digital Media Arts. Due to his academic standing, Elder Davon graduated with Magna Cum Laude honors for attaining a 3.7 GPA.

Elder Davon is a preacher of Holiness and a student of the word. His mission is to help others find their purpose in God while striving to meet the Lord face to face. Though he can be a forerunner in the pulpit, his greatest joy is seeing others strive to please God and fulfill their purpose according to the will of God. Also, he is a fantastic cook, brilliant artist, hilarious comedian, professional entrepreneur, and a kind and respectable person. Humility is his uniform and Integrity is his badge. Currently, Elder Davon serves as Elder and Director of Operations at Fresh Start Ministries with his mother, Pastor Cynthia Brown.

Elder Davon believes in the Spirit of Wisdom. In every aspect of his life, he lets wisdom take the lead. The scripture that God has sealed on his life comes from 1st Timothy 1:18-19, "This charge I commit unto thee, son Timothy, according to the prophecies which went before on thee, that thou by them mightest war a good warfare; Holding faith, and a good conscience; which some having put away concerning faith have made shipwreck."

Made in the USA
Middletown, DE
01 September 2024

60264277R00068